BREAKING FREE

Self-Reparenting
for
a New Life

Muriel James

BREAKING FREE

Self-Reparenting for a New Life

ADDISON-WESLEY PUBLISHING COMPANY

Reading, Massachusetts • Menlo Park, California
London • Amsterdam • Don Mills, Ontario • Sydney

First printing, August 1981
Second printing, October 1981
Third Printing, with corrections, November, 1981

Library of Congress Cataloging in Publication Data

James, Muriel.
  Breaking free.

  Includes index.
  1. Transactional analysis. 2. Success. 3. Parenting.
I. Title.
RC489.T7J353   158'.1   81–10767
ISBN 0–201–04664–4   AACR2
ISBN 0–201–04665–2 (pbk.)

ISBN 0-201-04665-2 P
ISBN 0-201-04664-4 H

CDEFGHIJ-DO-8987654321

OTHER BOOKS BY MURIEL JAMES
Published by Addison-Wesley

Born to Love: Transactional Analysis in the Church

Transactional Analysis for Moms and Dads: What Do You Do With Them
Now That You've Got Them?

Techniques in Transactional Analysis for Psychotherapists and Counselors

Marriage Is for Loving

The OK Boss

COAUTHORED WITH DOROTHY JONGEWARD
Born to Win: Transactional Analysis with Gestalt Experiments

Winning With People: Group Exercises in Transactional Analysis

The People Book: Transactional Analysis for Students

Winning Ways in Health Care

COAUTHORED WITH LOUIS SAVARY
A New Self: Self-Therapy with Transactional Analysis

Published by Harper and Row

The Power at the Bottom of the Well

The Heart of Friendship

This is in loving memory
of my mother and father,
Hazel and John Marshall,
who did the best
they knew how to do.

Acknowledgments

Over the years many people have parented me in many caring ways. Yet I wish to acknowledge the great debt I owe to a few important professors who may not know how much they meant to me: Robert Leslie, Jean and Sherman Johnson, Robert Beloof, Jack London, and Ward Tabler. In many important ways they served as substitute parents, encouraging me to think clearly, to take responsibility for my own learning and choices, and to do so in the social context of human suffering and the need to reduce it whenever possible.

I did not begin university studies until I was in my mid-thirties and at that time, in the mid-1950's, it was considered very unusual, even odd, for "a woman that old" to be starting as a freshman. These people helped me learn in a sometimes indifferent environment and grow in the process.

I also wish to thank Hope and John Arnot, who parented me by protecting me at a very critical period in my life, and Barbara Tabler, who taught me, when I and my children were almost starving during World War II, how to survive and to actually enjoy the surviving.

More currently I sing the praises of my long-time editor, Ann Dilworth of Addison-Wesley Publishing Company, for her great professional skill and personal involvement. When I became discouraged or frustrated with my sometimes inability to say what I wanted to say, she let me moan and groan. My friend, Betty Fielding, has done the same. In the process of writing this book, both have given me innumerable hours of help, have listened to my enthusiasms and complaints, and often helped me clarify my ideas. Then there are those to thank who have read all or part of the manuscript and given me important feedback: Maria Teresa Romanini, John James, Kathleen Kaulbach, Will Hardy, and Dave Owen. The ideas of each person have contributed to the book as a whole.

To my many friends and colleagues in the International Transactional Analysis Association, thank you. You have been interested, challenging, and supportive, and it has meant a great deal to me. And a special thanks to Kenneth Everts who first introduced me to TA, and to Eric Berne, its originator. I've been involved in the development of transactional analysis theory and its application since 1958 and have been expounding on the subject of self-reparenting for many years, even before my article about it was published in 1974 in the *Transactional Analysis Journal.* In fact, Martin Groder, who shared some of my time when I was under clinical supervision with Eric Berne, recently reminded me that I was arguing the theory of self-reparenting with Eric back in 1964. Obviously it has taken a long time for me to work through my original idea so that it could become a cohesive system that can be used by others.

Last, but definitely not least, I also owe a very special debt of gratitude to the many clients who came to me for psychotherapy and training. They contributed greatly to the development of this theory of self-reparenting and some of their case histories are in this book, naturally disguised. I thank them for their trust in me, for their commitment to themselves and to the excitement of change and breaking free.

Muriel James
Lafayette, California

Contents

Introduction

xix

1 Becoming Aware

1

What's Life All About, Anyway?
Born for Freedom
Feeling Trapped
Breaking Free
Discovering the Need
The Longing for Love
   Your Ideal Parent
A Personal Note
Notes from a Workshop
How About You?
Self-Reparenting: A Key to Freedom
A Good Parent? What's That?
Breakthrough I—Awareness and Freedom
   Born for Freedom
   Self Checklist
   A Freedom Continuum
   Journal Record

2
Temperament and
Personality   *21*

"My, How You've Grown!"
   Your Childhood Self-Image
Temperament Styles and the Lack of Freedom
A Personal Note
   Your Basic Temperament
The Three-Part Personality
Not-So-Good Parents
Notes from a Workshop
The Search for Roots
Breakthrough II—Personality Styles of Parents
   Your Use of Ego States
   Typical Negative Parenting
   Typical Positive Parenting
   Journal Record

3
Spellbound or
Free   *41*

Parents as Witches and Warlocks
The Magic of Spells
   Recognizing Spells
The Process of Spellbinding
Notes from a Workshop
   Waiting for a Spellbreaker
The Dumb and Ugly Club
Parental Spellbinding Injunctions
   Recognizing Injunctions
Spells of the Cultural Parent
   Cultural Spells
A Personal Note
Breakthrough III—Diagnosing Your Own Parents

Attributes of Your Parents
Positives and Negatives in Your Parent Ego State
Owning Your Parents
Journal Record

4
Adapting to
Authority   67

Parent Power
Notes from a Workshop
Obedience to Authority
   Learning to Obey
Styles of Obedience
Rebellion against Authority
   Choosing to Rebel
Procrastination Responses
Notes from a Workshop
   Procrastination as a Life-Style
Addictions to Life-Styles
Avoiding Freedom
The Morality of Obedience and Rebellion
Breakthrough IV—Comparing Life-Styles
   My Parents' Life-Style
   My Life-Style
   Evaluating Moral Decisions
   Excuses for Not Changing
   Journal Record

5
The Stress of
Unmet Needs   93

Needs and Wants Differ
Notes from a Workshop

Enslaved by Unmet Needs
   Your Childhood Needs and Wants
A System for Identifying Needs and Wants
   You and Your Needs
Stress and the Stress Response
Notes from a Workshop
   Needs, Wants, and Stress
The Stress of Memories
   Memories that Bless and Burn
The Stress of the Future
   Someday My Ship Will Come
The Stress of the Now
   The Now Experience
The New Parent and Stress Reduction
Notes from a Workshop
Breakthrough V—The Needs of the Child
   Dialogue with the Child
   Evaluating with the Adult
   Potency, Protection, and Permission
   Journal Record

6
Sources of Power

117

Expressions of Power
   Power and Your Child
The Loss of Power
   Energy Loss
Notes from a Workshop
Vitality and Physical Power
   Childhood Illness
Vitality in Spite of . . .
The Power of Personality
Notes from a Workshop

A Source of Power
The Power of Thinking
    Thinking and Problem Solving
Spiritual Power
    Transcendent Experiences
A Personal Note
Breakthrough VI—You and Your Power
    Vitality and Power
    Use and Misuse of Power
    Reparenting Your Powers
    Journal Record

7
Creating Strengths   *141*

Prerequisites to Creativity
Notes from a Workshop
    Learning to Wish
Logical and Creative Thinking
The Value of Intuition
    Your Intuition and Creativity
Vertical and Lateral Thinking
    Lateral Thinking for Problem Solving
Developmental Steps for Creating Strengths
Becoming an Artist
Amateurs versus Artists
Notes from a Workshop
Breakthrough VII—Breaking Through with Creativity
    Creative Writing
    Problem Area Quiz
    Strengths You Developed
    Strengths You Need
    Journal Record

8
Contracting for Freedom

165

Fidelity to Change
Determination and Will
   Your Developing Will
The Will-to-Power
   Your Childhood Will-to-Power
Notes from a Workshop
   Choosing to Change
Introduction to Contracting
The Process of Contracting
Notes from a Workshop
Other Contract Considerations
The Price of Caring
   The Price of Love and Care
Owning the Freedom to Change
Breakthrough VIII—Setting Contracts
   The Ayes and Nays
   Evaluating Contracts
   Ego States and Self-Sabotaging
   Sabotaging by Others
   Journal Record

9
From Hope to Joy

187

Is the Glass Half-Full or Half-Empty?
Notes from a Workshop
The Nature of Hope
   Your Use of Hope
Hope as Interpersonal Expectancy
   Disappointment and Hope

The Challenge to Forgive
  Forgiving Your Parents, Forgiving Yourself
From Satisfaction to Joy
  Your Experiences of Joy
Notes from a Workshop
The Importance of Play
  Let's Go Play
Laughter as a Road to Freedom
The Importance of Work
Notes from a Workshop
  Hope and Work
Choosing to Enjoy
  Your Enjoyment Style
From Joy to Happiness
For the Time Being
Celebrating Freedom
P.S. A Personal Thank-You
Certificate of Release

Bibliography   *213*
Index   *219*

Introduction

This book is about how to be a good parent to yourself. It offers you the theory of self-reparenting—what it is and why it is useful, and also the techniques for how to do it.

During the self-reparenting process, helping persons may be directly involved as therapists, teachers, guides, or allies. Yet the details will be up to you, you who believe it is important and creative to learn how to be a good parent to yourself.

For many years, I have been learning how to be a good parent to myself. I have also worked as a psychotherapist and educator with clients, counselees, and students, teaching them how to reparent themselves. I have been delighted with the immense change and growth that many people make when they learn how to be a good parent to themselves. Learning how to do this—in very specific ways—is constructive and productive. Although the process is a challenge, it's a healthy one because it enhances life. It is a sure path to freedom.

This book is a synthesis of many ideas. The word "synthesis" means the combining of separate elements to form a new unified whole. In some ways I envision this synthesis as a series of constantly changing patterns—life patterns that emerge and take shape, exist for a while and disappear. In some ways the colors and patterns of life are similar to those seen in a kaleidoscope that a person might pick up and turn while observing the changing designs made as the light shines on the bits of glass.

Some of the ideas about how to be a good parent to yourself will be closely connected, not requiring much rearrangement of the patterns. The connections of other ideas may be less obvious and the deeper implications for you may emerge slowly—perhaps as you just walk down the street thinking about who you are.

This is not a book on therapy and and techniques of Transactional Analysis (TA), as are many of my other books. However, it does use some of the valuable concepts for those who wish to see the relationships in a TA framework. *BREAKING FREE: Self-Reparenting for a New Life* is not written in a technical, academic style which sometimes impresses readers but also depresses them. It is written in everyday language for the thoughtful, interested reader who is personally involved in self-growth. It is also for my many peers and colleagues in the helping professions who enjoy theory and techniques that can be used to release people's awareness and increase their abilities to achieve more freedom and more integrity.

This book is for the thoughtful person, even the successful one who seeks even more inner freedom. It is for the person who wants to move and shape destiny, not be controlled by it. It is for the person who senses the need for more personal growth and is willing to commit some time and energy to reach this goal.

Many years ago I heard Alan Watts comment that many men and women tend to think in different ways. Men, he said, often have a "spotlight" approach to life. They focus in on an issue or problem. Women, in contrast, have "floodlight" vision. They perceive many necessary details that are not seen when only a spotlight is on.

Currently there is a widespread longing to experience what it means to expand the human potential. This expansion includes the awareness and use of both spotlight and floodlight ways of looking at life—either together or alternating in some creative pattern. Doing this increases people's chances to break free and to appreciate the complexities of becoming a new self.

Think for a moment of what it is like to attend a good drama production. As the actors portray their parts, there is usually a change in lighting. The spotlights may focus for a time, then be turned off so that the details on other parts of the stage become more noticeable to the audience.

So it is with breaking free. The light shed on life's problems and potentials can change—mellow or sharpen—according to the particular scene that is being observed.

Many people find it easier to observe the problems of others than their own problems. They may be like a passive audience to the drama of life rather than like leading characters or producers who can change the action and dialogue. This book is designed to encourage active change.

How the Book Can Help You

Throughout the book there are sections entitled "Notes from a Workshop." These notes are real-life case studies of persons who have been in self-reparenting training. Naturally the cases are disguised. Also included are brief but important awareness experiments. These are set into the book so that you can do them or ignore them. I hope you'll do them and discover more about yourself—what you need and how to get it. If you ignore them, it will be a little like painting the outside of a house when the foundation needs repair, or like using a handy-dandy list of techniques without knowing the basic philosophy and principles that undergird the techniques.

At the end of each chapter are very specific "Breakthrough" exercises that will involve you with yourself. These are in a logical sequence so that as you work through them, you will recognize how you are creating and developing a new sense of freedom for yourself.

The fact that you are reading this is a sign that you are interested in the subject. As you become even more interested in the process as well as the product, you may discover that keeping a journal would definitely be to your advantage. It is one of the most effective ways you can use to develop insight into who you are, where you've been, and where you might be going. Therefore you will find it useful to record, at the end of each chapter: what you have learned about your past self while studying the chapter, what you have learned about being a new, good parent to yourself, and what you have already done or can start doing now to further the process.

Many people fantasize that if they had only tried harder that they would have been able to win parents' love, acceptance, or approval. Many parents have the same fantasy that if they had only tried harder, their children would have naturally loved them more. Then when things go wrong in a family, as from time to time they usually do, both parents and children discover they are not perfect and may blame each other, so everyone ends up feeling miserable.

Some of you reading this book may have had responsible, understanding, and loving parents. Others may not have been so fortunate. In either case, this book will help you. In fact, I believe this so strongly that I offer you a guarantee. If you read it and do the exercises, then you will experience positive growth—even if you do or did have fine parents. After all, fine parents always want their children—whether young or grown up—to continue to grow. On the other hand, if you were unhappy or dissatisfied with the parenting you received, this will be an added bonus.

If you are a parent now, this book will help you be a better one. However, the specific focus is not on parenting others. It is on how to be a good parent to yourself. It is an exciting, productive, and healing process. You will discover a new source of inner power that may turn your life around.

This power will come as you restructure a part of your personality so that you become a good parent to yourself—not repressive nor critical nor indifferent nor indulgent, indecisive, or inconsistent, but a good parent to you. The kind you need to have in your life *now*.

Of course your own parents may have had many positive qualities. I hope so; they're a part of you now which you may or may not be aware of. Yet didn't you then, or don't you now, wish they had been somewhat different? Taken better care of themselves and you? Listened to you better? Lived longer? Loved you more?

If so, then these qualities that you wish they had are qualities that you can develop for yourself. When you do, you will like yourself better, have more friends, be more pleased with success, be physically and emotionally healthier, and, I guarantee, you will experience more joy in your day-to-day living. All this because you will become a good parent to yourself.

Breaking Free with Self-Reparenting

The process of self-reparenting is a challenging task that takes time and commitment. A brief overview of the process will serve as an introductory guide.

In the first chapter, some of the issues of freedom are raised. What is unlimited freedom? Why do so many people feel trapped? How does the process of breaking free begin? These and other materials are intended to increase the awareness of the need most people have for a new kind of positive parent.

The second chapter is concerned with categories of inborn temperament, with an understanding of personality structure and what constitutes not-so-good parents. The seven more common types of parenting styles are presented, and you will discover how these styles can be negative or positive and what you need for yourself.

In the third chapter the effect of spellbinding parents, or other parent figures such as teachers, is explored. The power of injunctions, given verbally or non-verbally, is examined. Furthering the process of breaking free by analyzing the positive and negative parenting in one's personal life is the goal of this chapter.

The next focus is how people tend to respond to authority by patterns of obedience, rebellion, and procrastination. The rational or irrational authority of parents often teach people compulsive behaviors which become life-styles. Like addictions, characteristic ways of responding are hard to give up. Comparing personal with parental life-styles becomes a focus in the breaking-free exercise.

The needs people have and how they create stress is the subject of the fifth chapter. Also included are ways to analyze personal needs. When these needs are not met, there is an increase in the stress responses. Sometimes personal needs are in conflict with personal desires. The reconciliation of needs and desires is a breakthrough to freedom.

Without freedom, the use and abuse of power increases or decreases motivation that leads to change. This sixth chapter is about four kinds of power: physical power that comes with vitality, personality power, intellectual power, and spiritual power. If these powers are used, the sense of freedom grows and continues until death. If these powers are misused, they become problems that are "recycled" in later life. The new Parent you learn to develop can help you channel your power for freedom.

In the next chapter, the focus is on creativity and how it develops with the use of intuition and other strengths. These strengths may or may not follow the normal course of development. Becoming a new parent to oneself is an act of creation. It requires an artist's dedication and leads to a sense of confidence and well-being.

With confidence, people establish goals designed to increase their freedom. They establish procedures and learn how to make contracts for achieving their goals. The techniques in chapter eight on making contracts can be used in any and every area of life. Learning how to do this can become a valuable asset.

The conclusion of learning this process of self-reparenting is an always fresh experience of breaking free. Breaking free leads to the discovery of joy, and joy is much more than satisfaction. Breaking free also leads to awareness of how to be happy. All of these are goals of this book.

Becoming Aware

1

"Know thyself?"
If I knew myself, I'd run away.
Goethe

To become aware of life is to become excited by its potential. It is to become aware of experiences of love and beauty, of work and achievement, of pain and suffering, and to affirm the meaning of it all even when, on occasion, it seems meaningless.

Many people are excited by life. They find meaning in their experiences of beauty, their achievements that lead to success, even in their struggles to discover who they are and what it's all about.

Other people are bored with life. Or angry with life. Or despairing about life. They beat themselves up, let themselves down, deny themselves pleasure, keep themselves captive, refuse themselves the chance to grow. They do not allow themselves to find meaning or permit themselves to break free.

The first type of person believes in the meaning of freedom and knows what it's like to experience joy. The second type of person does not experience freedom and instead feels trapped and miserable or, at best, indifferent.

The search for meaning is a lifelong journey. It is part of the search for personal identity and joy. Yet knowing oneself is a scary idea to many people.

They may want to know about their minds but not their bodies or spirit. Or they may want to understand what goes on in their bodies, and at the same time they may deny or ignore the effect their emotions have on them,

Many people are afraid to know themselves because they imagine they might discover something awful. I believe that at a deeper level they are afraid they might discover something awesome and wonderful. Discovering "something wonderful" is scary because it presents a strong challenge—the challenge to live up to the awesome wonder of being oneself and to take charge of one's own life.

"Know thyself" was the advice given to each person who entered the ancient Greek temple at Delphi. Yet the search for self-knowledge began much earlier. Ancient paintings and sculpture reveal the growing awareness of mortality and the search for meaning and transcendence when acknowledging that fact.

People find meaning in different ways. Some, for example, find meaning in their bodies and its beauty or strength. In the process of physical exercise such as jogging they may become more aware of who they are. Others find meaning when using their brains in intellectual pursuits or academic achievements. Others find meaning in positive accomplishments that lead to power, prestige, or possession, or to self-satisfaction for a job well done. Michelangelo's ceiling of the Sistine Chapel shows part of his struggle to know himself through his art. Hugh Hefner's *Playboy* presents a different point of view. Both are valid, yet the messages and meanings differ.

What is meaningful at one time in a person's life may have little meaning later. The drive for financial security may lose its meaning if terminal illness becomes imminent. The dedication to a family may lose its meaning if constant criticism occurs. The involvement in a job or school may lose its meaning to a person falling in love. The struggle for prestige may lose its meaning if nobody is impressed. Old meanings are then given up with comments such as, "It doesn't mean anything to me any more."

What's Life All About, Anyway?

This lifelong search for meaning rests on two deceptively simple questions: "Who am I?" and "What am I doing here?"

People who ask themselves, "Who am I?" often respond with a list of nouns such as "a mother," "an artist," "a secretary," "a student," and of adjec-

Who Am I?

"I wonder, who am I?"

"What does it all mean?"   "And who am I?"

tives—"a tired mother," "a frustrated artist," "a competent secretary," or "a good student." Often these words refer to what they do rather than who they are—a finite human being who once upon a time was born and who once upon a time will die and who will live between those two events and use, more or less, inherent and developed potentials.

People who ask themselves, "What am I doing here?" may respond with verb phrases that reflect high, low, or no concern for growth in self-awareness. Common phrases are "If I knew what was right to do, I would do it," "I don't know what I'm doing," and "Who cares what I'm doing?"

When the questions are asked with the emphasis on *I*, "Who am *I*?" "What am *I* doing here?" the answers sometimes lead to new awareness for the need to change. Change often requires courage—the courage to *be* who you are, to affirm your human existence—and the courage to *do* what seems the most human. Being and doing are basic categories that can bring meaning and newness and excitement to anyone's life. Many don't allow this to happen because they think of themselves as trapped. Often they are.

Although people occasionally free themselves from some of the economic, social, and political forces that control their lives, many who do so then turn around and choose new kinds of enslavement. For example, repressive marriages, or jobs, that enslave and control are psychological parallels to the authoritarian governments they or their ancestors may have fought in the past.

Because freedom is so often confused with a license to "do your own thing," the word and concepts need continual evaluation. "Doing your own thing" is not necessarily a sign of autonomy. It is often an act of rebellion against real or imagined authority figures. When this is the case, the person is not free but is more like a three-year-old child having temper tantrums while trying to manipulate his or her world with an impotent show of anger.

The real sense of freedom is deep in a person's inner core. It is not an *illusion* of individuality; it is the *reality* of it.

Born for Freedom

People are not born free, yet they are born for freedom. They are born for freedom because *freedom is part of being human*. In any situation there usually is some freedom for the body and for the mind. In rare situations where bodily freedom may not exist, such as when a person is in an iron lung, a person's mind often takes flight, in thought or in fantasy. Even when brainwashed, some part of a person's spirit is free, non-confined, and non-confinable, and this inner sense of freedom may be experienced in spite of any external bars and barriers if a person finds meaning in existence.

Viktor Frankl, writing of his experiences in concentration camps during World War II, demonstrates how finding meaning leads to freedom in spite of seemingly intolerable situations. He and a group of other physicians formed a medical association that met in secret. This association, concerned as it was with medical theory and practices, also encouraged freedoms within their group—freedom of personal thought and freedom to find creative ways to survive. Survival often involves flexible thinking and creative changes. Dinosaurs did not adapt to change and look what happened to them! Fossils!

Freedom that a person is born with includes the *freedom to change oneself and the world.* Change may have limits but freedom to change does not. Although some people resign themselves to situations and refuse to change or complain that they "can't" change, at the inner core of their being they cannot escape this human capacity. The freedom to change is a "given."

Another given is the *freedom to observe oneself while in the process of change.* "When I stop for a moment," said Robert, "I usually see what I'm doing." "Yeah, me too," Mary chimed in. "I often feel as if I'm outside myself, watching."

Another part of being human is *freedom to think and decide what is important and what needs changing.* So is the capacity to go freely against one's healthy decisions and give in to greed, hostility, compulsiveness, and illness.

When people exercise their freedoms in negative ways, they may often find themselves filled with inner anxieties for doing so. Yet even when filled with anxiety over what they have or have not done, or even when filled with despair over something that is incurable or changeless, people are free to change their attitudes and thus to change their emotional environment.

Thus, the capacity for freedom, "in spite of . . . " is as real as the capacity to breathe. Like breath, freedom may be restricted, even shallow. It cannot be lost, not until death. The lifelong search to experience freedom is at the deepest core of being. It is an urge that motivates people to break out of their misery. Freedom gives meaning to life and people are born for freedom.

Feeling Trapped

The sense of feeling trapped is a familiar one, as any motorist on a crowded freeway will tell you. The feeling can permeate all areas of life. Too many papers on a crowded desk, too many children in a crowded room, too many requests, and too much to do all lead to frustration and to the desire to break free.

In many situations, to fight against being trapped or to flee from it can be a healthy response. The unhealthy response is resignation and apathy. A person who feels trapped might say: "What difference does it make? Nothing means anything anyway." Discouraged and depressed, hopeless and helpless, without goals or dreams of freedom, the person *feeling* trapped begins to *act* trapped.

This pattern often has its beginning in early childhood. Freedom to explore and play may be severely restricted by parents. Freedom to think independently may be restricted by teachers acting as parent substitutes. Freedom to hope and trust may be destroyed because of a hopeless environment.

In any case, the childhood sense of feeling trapped may lead to a lifetime filled with a sense of inadequacy and little joy. Procrastinating and claiming to be unable to make decisions may become a life-style.

Some people do not feel this seriously trapped. They do not experience their frustration at such a deep level, or if they do, it is only occasional rather than frequent. Yet even these people sometimes need to escape and express their frustration with comments such as:

"I *can't* seem to get away from people who talk on and on."

"I *can't* ever get away from my kids."

"I *can't* say no to a woman."

"I *can't* manage my time."

"I *can't* seem to save any money."

"I *can't* make friends."

Any time the word *can't* is used, the person using it feels trapped.

Breaking Free

Literature and lives are full of situations that people choose to stay trapped in rather than risk breaking free. One of the Old Testament stories is about the ancient Israelites who were imprisoned in Egypt some four hundred years. When they escaped, crossing what was called the Red Sea under the leadership of Moses, they were confused and unhappy. Many wanted to return to their captors. Under captivity they knew what to expect and how to survive. Freedom was difficult medicine to take. It took courage, hope, will, and purpose to become autonomous. It took more of the same, plus competency, fidelity, love, and caring to remain free.

Three thousand years later in Germany, Martin Luther, the so-called Father of the Reformation, translated the Bible and editorialized on this story. He wrote, "What else is our whole life on earth than a passing through the Red Sea?"

This comment "crossing the Red Sea" means that people assume courageous responsibility for who they are (their "being") and how they live their lives (their "doing"). It implies that all life is a process of coming out from slavery imposed by culture, by outdated mores, by lack of information, by manipulative people, or by any number of restrictive encounters—including those with parents. Crossing the Red Sea is a symbol of the road to freedom.

The word *freedom* poses a dilemma: freedom *from* what? freedom *to* what? Freedom is struggle because it brings new responsibilities, new dimensions. Change may, or may not, lead to freedom; freedom invariably leads to change. It is not license or the liberty to do anything one wants. No. Freedom is liberation from slavery, imprisonment, or restraint.

All people experience a lack of freedom—physical, emotional, social, and so forth. Many *seem* to prefer it rather than risk change, with potential failure. Yet I believe that in spite of their fear or anxiety, people really want freedom, and freedom is possible when people develop their capacities for being good parents to themselves. This may seem like an odd notion to those who are grown up and may not sense the need for parents or may not be aware of how their parents and culture limited their sense of freedom.

With many parents freedom *is not* encouraged, obedience is. The obedience desired is the families' traditions, life-styles, or standards of behavior—ways of thinking, acting, and feeling. With other parents, freedom to be independent *is* encouraged. Yet even when this is the case, the effects of the larger culture may encourage or interfere with breaking free.

In many Eastern cultures the sense of individual freedom has not been encouraged. Social solidarity, usually in the family unit, has been stressed. In Western cultures the desire for individual freedom has been growing since the Renaissance. Patterns of migration and immigration reflect the urge to

What am I doing here?

"Symbols of freedom
still attract."

"Free, but no place to go."

"Freedom, not slavery,
is everyone's right."

"Breaking free is not easy."

break free. At the present time there is a new undercurrent, in the East for more individual freedom, in the West for unity and oneness with others.

Both movements reflect a breaking free from tradition, the development of an inner parent who encourages the search for freedom—how to recognize it, expand it, develop it, and use it responsibly. When people become good parents to themselves they feel an inner sense of liberation and joy.

Discovering the Need

On one occasion while I was writing this book, I had dinner with a young couple I know very well. They were experiencing a great deal of stress concerning their children, their finances, and their jobs.

In a sudden effort to change the subject, the man turned to me and asked, "Are you writing any more books?" I told him about my research on self-reparenting and how the focus of this book would be how to be a good parent to yourself.

At those words a look of despair passed over his face. Although he seldom showed feelings, at this moment his vulnerability was clear and the words poured out, "Oh, wow, if I only knew how to be a good parent to myself. All my hard work won't mean much if I kill myself with a heart attack by working too hard like my father did. My family needs me and I need them. Furthermore *I want to find out who I am before it's too late.*"

Everyone needs some degree of self-reparenting, yet not everyone is aware of that need. The motivation to become a good parent to yourself may develop slowly over a long period of time, or rapidly, as when a crisis occurs. People are motivated to explore self-reparenting for different reasons. Some because they feel unimportant or unloved, as if their existence doesn't make any difference. Some because they feel valueless unless they act as workaholics. Others feel secure only when they are taking care of others or being taken care of. There are many other reasons because the human condition is that everyone needs freedom-loving and joyful parents, and they seem to be in short supply.

The Longing for Love

We seldom give up our longing for loving parents. Even a loving spouse or friend cannot fill the role. Without two loving parents children suffer—some greatly, some to a lesser degree. They feel as if they lack something; it is as if they have a hole inside. When they grow up they may have a magical belief of what they would have been like if only they had had ideal parents. Sometimes the fantasy gives them emotional support and a sense of direction. Sometimes they use it as an excuse for doing nothing.

Recently some people who were taking a self-reparenting workshop explored their fantasies of an ideal parent. The question posed was, "How would you be different if you had had ideal parents?" Some of their responses were:

"I'd be much more relaxed and easygoing instead of anxious and pressured."

"I'd be respected and popular instead of unhappy and screwed up."

"I'd be free to choose instead of locked in like I am now."

"I'd be living out my dreams instead of just doing what I'm 'supposed' to do."

"I'd be integrated and together instead of scattered and falling apart."

"I'd be more nurturing and touching instead of so critical and distant."

"I'd have more fun instead of being so uptight."

"I'd be more decisive instead of afraid to make up my mind."

The dream of the ideal parent is a common one because of a basic longing for love. Being loved and lovable is a universal desire.

Your Ideal Parent

Experiment with this initial awareness exercise. First let yourself relax deeply. Then consider: What would you be like now if you had had ideal parents? Also, what would you do?

Would you be different than you were when you were younger? Or would you tend to be the same?

Do you need to learn how to be a loving parent to yourself? If so, what small beginning can you make now? Don't rush into a decision. Just sit and meditate on it for a while.

A Personal Note

My own awareness of the self-reparenting process started with some unhappiness about my own parents. Although my mother and father were very caring, responsible parents in many ways, I cannot remember if they ever *asked* me how I felt. Feelings weren't talked about. Nor did they touch me much, as far as I can remember. Yet being touched can be healing and being asked, "How are you?" is affirming. I decided I needed both so I figured out how to get other people to treat me in those ways. First I started asking them how they felt while encouraging them to ask me how I felt. Next, I observed the many ways they touched others and I experimented in a like manner. I started touching other people and my own children more. I also made some new friends, people who were warm and not afraid to touch and who cared about how I felt.

In the beginning this new touching and talking about feelings felt uncomfortable and strange, like trying to balance on a tightrope or like being a stranger in an unknown country. Eventually it became automatic and I did it without thinking. Unknowingly the behavior had become part of my new parent, an ideal inner parent who would give me what I wanted.

I didn't know that I was also giving my new parent to other people until some years later when I had a most interesting experience. I had just led a two-day workshop for upper-management personnel of a large corporation, and I was driven to the airport by one of the participants whom I did not know by name or otherwise. Instead of expressing cordial appreciation or a warm, excited, childlike "Oh, thank you so much," I suddenly hugged this stranger and tenderly asked, "How are you?" in a very caring, parental way. Imagine his surprise, meeting this new parent in me at this moment. Some people wouldn't have liked it; fortunately he did.

Since then I've been more aware. What *I* need to do to be a good parent to myself is not always appropriate to use on someone else. Each person needs to decide independently what a new parent needs to be.

Notes from a Workshop

Cynthia claimed to have had a "perfect" childhood with "perfect" parents. She entered the self-reparenting workshop expressing confusion because of the behavior of her husband of one year and of some of the new friends they were making in the community. "They act so rude!" she complained. "They interrupt all the time. Each one wants to talk more than the other. I don't understand people like that! I can't be friends with them. It wasn't that way where I came from. I just can't stand it. In fact my shoulders get really up-tight and I get a stomachache just thinking about it. I love my husband but I feel like leaving him and going back home right now."

Cynthia's conscientious, protective, polite, well-mannered parents had not prepared her for the world that is not always polite. Nor had they prepared her to evaluate behavior—what is important and what is not. She had learned only to judge what was "right" or "wrong" according to their standards and consequently had few friends. Cynthia needed a new inner parent who would encourage her to be flexible rather than rigid, to think analytically for herself rather than continue with her parental prejudices, to relax her standards so that her body could relax. Then she could enjoy her-self, her husband, and other people more.

Tony didn't like her. Within the first hour of the workshop he lashed out, "You look just like my mother and I can't stand it. You're even shaped the same way, and your eyes and hair are the same color as hers. There're other women at work with the same appearance and I can't stand them, either. They're always out to get you. You're not free. They manipulate you with their eyes and bodies and there you are—stuck."

Of course Tony was stuck. He was "stuck" with his childhood decisions about his mother and projecting this onto women in general. Tony had to work hard to change the way he used his memories of this childhood parent as an excuse for getting angry. An ulcer that his physician said was related to psychological problems was the symptom that brought Tony to therapy. Recognizing his need to change was not easy. It required courage.

Eli had a different problem. Though awake, his eyes were often closed or half-closed. Only rarely did he look directly at people. Eli rarely spoke. He did not initiate conversation and responded politely only when spoken to. When small-group discussions during the workshop were going on, Cynthia often sought him out to complain about others. Her self-righteousness and verbal diarrhea was commented on by another group member. Her defensive retort was, "Yes, but I'm not interrupting him be-cause he's not talking."

People's senses are interrelated. When they shut their ears, they may not *see;* when they shut their eyes, they may not *hear.* Eli had both seeing and hearing problems. As a child he had tuned out his parents' continual bicker-ing and faultfinding and did not see what was going on. As a very little boy he had learned to squeeze his eyes tightly shut in the magical belief that he wouldn't hear them.

Maria, who joined the same workshop, came from a very different background. Deserted by her mother, brutalized by her alcoholic father, Maria had few social graces, only an undying determination to get out of her dehumanizing environment and succeed. The new inner parent she needed would be one that would not desert her or cop out when faced with unhappiness or frustration.

The self-reparenting process was difficult for Maria. Often she would become emotionally upset when talking about what it was like when she was a little girl. Then she would become fearful that someone in the group would attack her. At the same time she would panic that they would leave and she would be left alone, deserted once more as she had been in childhood. Maria was able to develop a new, responsible, protective inner parent. In time she learned how to control and finally give up those old feelings, which were related to the past and not to the here and now. She developed a new good parent for herself.

How About You?

Some people are so accustomed to being who they are and doing what they do that they do not stop to think about how free they would feel if they learned how to be a good parent to themselves. The need for being a better parent to oneself often shows in physical symptoms. One way to start thinking about breaking free is to consider the following questions. Then you can find out how you need to be a better parent to yourself. Start with physical symptoms.

Do you take care of yourself and are you generally healthy, or do you have headaches or stomachaches or backaches? Are you overweight or underweight? Is your blood pressure too high or too low? Do you tire easily or often feel deeply fatigued? Do you sleep well and wake refreshed, or do you have difficulty sleeping and often toss and turn for hours?

Physical symptoms are not the only signs of the need for reparenting yourself. When you frequently experience unpleasant emotions such as fear, anger, guilt, or depression, or when a pervading sense of anxiety about not being able to think clearly or solve problems or achieve goals interferes with your happiness, you also need self-reparenting. Some of the questions you can ask yourself to determine if your feelings interfere with your sense of freedom are: Do you often feel like an outsider in new social situations? Feel awkward or unattractive or shy or tongue-tied and don't know what to say and therefore avoid meeting new people? Do you respect yourself and con-gratulate yourself for your values and achievements, or do you feel a sense of low self-esteem? Do you see yourself as autonomous and free, able to de-velop your skills and interests, or do you feel somewhat trapped? Do you usually forgive yourself when you make errors or get criticized or are re-jected in some way, or do you sometimes "beat up on yourself"? Do you have friends and family whom you enjoy and with whom you can be open, or are you kind of lonely? Are you involved with the larger world than just your family, friends, and colleagues, or have you given up on much of the human race and perhaps become indifferent? Do you often feel an inner sense of confidence and peace, as well as a high excitement and delight in living, or do you often feel insecure and perhaps in turmoil?

Perhaps your answers to these questions were strongly on the positive side. If so, you may not need self-reparenting. So give this book to a friend or colleague or client or family member, or even to a stranger.

Perhaps your answers were less strong yet still positive. If so, you need to be a good parent to yourself to reinforce and develop what is already posi-tive.

And if you had several negative answers, you need this process—for sure—so that you can break free for a new life.

Self-Reparenting: A Key to Freedom

We all had parents. Sometimes our parents may have been tender, positive, thoughtful, and creative. Other times our parents may have been critical, overprotective, inconsistent, conflicting, uninvolved, overorganized, or emotionally dependent. For better and worse we incorporated the parenting we received in childhood into our personalities. Unknowingly we use this "old parent" on ourselves and others. It needs to be updated so that each of us can be a better, more loving parent to ourselves on a day-to-day basis. When self-reparenting is complete, you will be more affirming of life, have higher self-esteem, solve problems more effectively, enjoy life at deeper levels, and taste the ambrosia of happiness more often.

The idea of reparenting is not new. Since the beginning of time, persons have acted as substitute parents to others—with or without awareness.

Women have done this more frequently than men. Yet men have also assumed parenting functions. Fiction and nonfiction, ancient and contemporary history, are full of examples of grandparents, aunts, uncles, older siblings, even friends who act as substitute parents. Even an institution may have this role.

In many cases, these people have such an influence that their values and lifestyles become part of the personalities of their charges. In essence, they have *reparented* them.

Self-reparenting is different from reparenting. Self-reparenting is a new theory with very specific procedures based on a personal decision to become a new parent to oneself. That means learning how to take charge of your life—turning it around if need be. Breaking free to live a new life.

A brief glimpse of the process shows a series of eight steps. First comes the awareness that something seems to be missing within. That something missing is a nurturing parent who encourages freedom, autonomy, and joy. The second step is a reflection on parents in general, the parenting styles most commonly used, and the kinds of responses that are commonly made. Third comes the analysis of our own parenting figures. These figures, for better or worse, are incorporated into the personality structure. The fourth step is discovering what the inner-child part of us needs and wants.

The fifth step is clarifying the various sources of personal power you can mobilize so that you can respond to your needs and wants. Next comes the awareness of strengths or virtues you have already developed, or need to develop, that will assist you in creating a new self-parent. Then comes the time for learning how to make contracts with yourself that will enhance your life. The eighth and last step is positive reinforcement because of newfound courage to break free. You'll have a new, good, loving parent within who will treat you with dignity, respect, and care. You'll have new hope, new joy, new happiness.

A Good Parent? What's That?

Developing a new good parent is a problem without a clear definition of the word *good.* I recently asked my eight-year-old grandson what he thought a bad person was like. He said with great emphasis, "A bad person is boring!" When I asked what a good person was like, he looked at me with amazement, saying, "But Grandma, everyone knows what a good person is like. Don't you?" I said I wasn't sure. To me, trying to define the word *good* is a little like trying to count the number of angels dancing on the head of a pin.

It can't be done because the concept of what makes up a good parent differs from person to person. In spite of the difficulty, there is some general agreement that it refers to having desirable qualities. Then the question is, What is desirable? Along with that is, What is possible?

A good parent usually provides for a child's basic physical and safety needs. In some situations and cultures this is not easy, and a child may grow up malnourished and fearful.

A good parent loves the child, and the child, in response, has a sense of belongingness. In some situations this is not easy. If the parent feels personally unhappy and unable to love, the child grows up feeling like an unloveable person—an outsider.

A good parent esteems and respects the child. In some cases this is not easy if the child does not conform to parental standards or if a parent is so emotionally needy that she or he has little tolerance for children's problems and little willingness to applaud their successes. Then a child often grows up feeling unable to please others because of low self-esteem.

A good parent encourages freedom and self-actualization. That may not be easy. Many parents have not had that experience for themselves and may not even know such things are possible. The child may grow up without awareness or interest in issues that involve truth and justice, or beauty and joy.

What else is the function of a good parent? Certainly to provide a home, the kind of place that Robert Frost describes: "Home is a place that when you have to go there, they have to take you in." A good parent provides that kind of place of sanctuary and solace. When the world seems to stop turning on its axis; when favorite dreams become nightmares and lovers become ogres; when power, prestige, and possessions are empty substitutes for love; then home is needed—home with a welcome mat before the door. And one of the functions of being a good parent is to lay out the welcome mat.

Yet not only to provide a place where you can go when no one else will have you. Not just a haven when things go wrong. A good parent also provides a problem solving situation and a place where love is high—higher than a kite, than a flock of Canadian geese flying north, higher than the stars in the Milky Way. And you need to have that kind of parent—a good parent—as a part of your personality.

Breakthrough I—Awareness and Freedom

The following exercises are designed to bring into your awareness your need for breaking free. You may do them slowly and thoughtfully or you may ignore, for the time, those with which you feel very uncomfortable.

Born for Freedom   Go to a quiet place; sit down in a comfortable chair. Take a few deep breaths and let your memory drift back in time.

What, if anything, was said about your birth? About being who you are? About being born for freedom?

How were you encouraged to be dependent, independent, or interdependent?

In what specific ways did you feel your freedom was inhibited by your family; that is, could you go where you wanted to go, have friends over to your house, think your own thoughts, have your own interests?

In what ways did you hold yourself back? In what ways do you hold yourself back now and deny yourself freedom?

Self Checklist   Look quickly at the following list. Put a checkmark (√) beside those that you apply to yourself. Use a cross (X) for those that do not apply to you. Use a question mark (?) for those you are unsure about.

____Don't understand myself	____Usually give in to others
____Don't take care of myself	____Often happy
____Independent thinker	____Feel trapped
____Give up easily on goals	____Well liked
____Often rebellious	____Too critical
____Good health	____Creative

Born to be Free

James

National Archives

"Good morning, world."

"We're free to go see."

"Does it want to be free?"

"I'm free to be me, or am I?"

National Archives   Hebble

____Basically hopeful	____Glad to be alive
____Poor self-control	____Feel incomplete
____Often feel guilty	____Good at problem solving
____Wish I'd never been born	____Feel free
____Not too good as a parent	____Overly nurturing
____Don't like myself	____Competent
____Think I'm OK	____Trust myself
____Procrastinate often	____Weak instead of powerful
____Very competitive	____Children like me
____No close friends	____Frequently I don't understand

Look at your marks on the checklist.

Is there a pattern? Are you trapped in certain ways and free in others?

If you had had an ideal parent, how would you have been different?

A Freedom Continuum   When you consider various aspects of your life, how would you rate yourself on the following continuums?

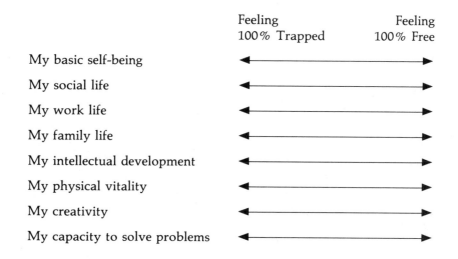

	Feeling 100% Trapped	Feeling 100% Free
My basic self-being	◄―――――――――►	
My social life	◄―――――――――►	
My work life	◄―――――――――►	
My family life	◄―――――――――►	
My intellectual development	◄―――――――――►	
My physical vitality	◄―――――――――►	
My creativity	◄―――――――――►	
My capacity to solve problems	◄―――――――――►	

	Feeling 100% Trapped	Feeling 100% Free
My personality	◄───────────────────────────►	
My use of time	◄───────────────────────────►	
My intimate relationships	◄───────────────────────────►	

Are there other categories you would add to this list? If so, you're *free* to do so. Even to write in the book—that is, if it's your book!

Your journal is for you to use. Record what you think and feel about who you are and what you're doing and how you are working on breaking free.

Temperament
and Personality

2

*There is as much difference between us and ourselves as
between us and others.*

Montaigne

Differences in people are often recognized, but seldom are they celebrated.
Many people don't like differences. They want other people to be like themselves. Even if they don't think much of themselves, they often expect others
to fit into some imaginary ideal mold of what "should" be.

The differences in people start at birth. Some babies are more active than
others; some cry more; some sleep more. These basic temperaments form a
significant part of each person's self-image and personality.

In order to incorporate a "good parent" into your personality, you may
need to understand your self better, that is, how and why you have grown
to be the person you are. The next eight chapters of this book will help you
do that. This chapter will show you how your personality has developed by
looking at your basic temperaments and your parents' reactions to them.

"My, How You've Grown!"

Many children have the experience of hearing the words, "My, how you've
grown!" from a relative or family friend who has not seen them for a long
time. The words often create a sense of embarrassment in children, who

may want to be noticed for reasons other than size. They may think to themselves, "Well, of course I've grown—what did they expect!" The self-image children have usually includes the belief that they will grow taller. It sometimes includes the belief that they will grow more competent. It rarely includes the belief that they will grow more loveable. That decision is made very early in life.

Most people base their self-image on early childhood beliefs about who they are and what they could or should be doing. These childhood beliefs are usually determined on the basis of how their parents treated them when they were young. At times, parents emphasize children's basic existence, their *being,* either negatively or positively:

"Just who do you think you are, young man!"

"Go away. I wish I'd never had you."

"You're what I always wanted."

"You're a great kid."

At other times parents emphasize a child's *doing,* his or her behavior, either negatively or positively:

"You never do anything right; you're so clumsy."

"I told you! Watch out what you're doing!"

"You're very creative with your hands."

"You finished that very well."

Your Childhood Self-Image

Sit down quietly and let your memory drift back in time to when you were a child.

What was your self-image as a human being?

What was your self-image about what you should or could do?

Do you still have these basic self-images?

How do they affect your total self-image now?

Temperament Styles and the Lack of Freedom

As people get older, their beliefs may be modified, sometimes by other parent figures, yet the original questions of being and doing—"Who am I?" and "What am I doing here?"—often remain throughout life. They can be answered, in part, by considering temperament. Temperament and personality are not the same. A person's temperament refers to the characteristic way that particular person behaves and reacts because of their genetic inheritance. The study of temperament is the study of behavioral styles—*how* people do what they do. It does not focus on *what* a person does, or *why*, but on *how*. Personality is a larger term; it includes temperament but is not limited to it. The study of personality is also concerned with how people develop in response to life experiences, what they do and often why.

Many parents do not know that children are born with a specific temperament style. They may know that eye and hair color is genetically determined yet be unaware that a child's disposition is also a genetic factor.

Some children are difficult to be around—difficult for themselves and others. Some are easy to be around—easy on themselves and on others. In either case they may repel or attract others, often because of their temperament, yet they may not know what the factors are. If they do not know themselves, then it is painful to figure out how to break free.

Anyone who has watched a group of newborn infants can easily see that they behave differently, for example, in their sleeping and eating patterns, in their responses to other people, and in the amount and kind of movement they display. Many researchers in child development have described some of the unique differences. One of the most interesting pieces of research was developed by Alexander Thomas, Stella Chess, and Herbert Birch. They conducted an in-depth study on a group of 136 infants from birth to adult life. Although there are many studies about people, this is one of the few longitudinal studies. As a result of their findings, the researchers concluded that temperament, genetically transmitted, may remain unchanged through life or it may be strengthened or diminished by environmental circumstances. Recent studies on identical twins reached similar conclusions, and additional research shows striking differences in temperament in different ethnic groups.

Because temperament is part of a person's genetic structure, it is seemingly unrelated to birth order, health, or intelligence. Yet it can be modified. To modify it requires an awareness of the nine basic temperament styles. These may be combined in different ways and each can contribute to and interfere with freedom.

Activity level refers to mobility. Some children move a lot when sleeping, wiggle and squirm a lot when awake, tire others out by their constant movement, have a high activity level. "Gee, he's an always-active kid," a parent might exclaim. The very physically active are a strong contrast to those who are more placid, who lie quietly and move slowly and, to many parents, are easier to care for. "He's so easygoing," one parent might say approvingly. Other parents, with a high activity level themselves, might become very impatient with a slow-moving child.

When grown up, the high-activity person is likely to have high energy and prefer work that allows for considerable bodily movement. This person is not satisfied with sitting in a chair for long periods of time and thus may be frustrated with a child who is more placid and relaxed.

Rhythm is the second temperamental characteristic and refers to the regularity of biological functions—sleeping and waking, eating and defecating. Children who are predictable, who seem to have a regular natural rhythm, are usually preferred by parents to those who don't. "I can count on Pete to always go to the bathroom at 7:00 A.M., but not Mary—she's unpredictable."

This regularity of biological rhythm contributes to the predictable schedule this person, when grown up, prefers to keep. If for some reason the schedule is upset, this person may feel very upset, even sick.

Approach or withdrawal response is the temperament category used to describe a child's initial reaction to anything new—new foods, new toys, new people. "He likes to go to new places" refers to a child who, by temperament, approaches many facets of life rather than withdrawing from them. Curious, often an extroverted type, this child quickly feels at home in new situations. The opposite type is the one who prefers the routine and familiar, and resists new experiences.

When grown up, persons who approach new situations easily may enjoy jobs that frequently require new "customer contact," or involvement of some kind with new products. They may resent routine that does not allow for newness and change.

Adaptability refers to the initial ease and speed with which people can change their behavior when faced with new or changed situations. "She's so shy" may be said about a child with low adaptability who makes friends slowly and takes a long time to adjust. "She's so friendly" may be said about a child with high adaptability to strangers.

People who get along easily with many others because of their high level of adaptability are somewhat like the persons with the previous temperament style. However, their focus is on adaptability to the people already within their environment rather than reaching out to new people and new experiences.

Intensity of reaction can be positive or negative. Some children are very intense. They may "devour" their food, try to overwhelm their parents with temper tantrums, respond forcefully, scream with delight. They are usually considered "very excitable." Those with a low intensity of reaction respond more softly, are more passive, may not easily express their feelings. When two children with opposite intensity reactions are together, one may bully the other. When two are together with high intensity, they may frequently fight or become passionately involved in some "cause."

When grown up, an intense person sometimes resents those who are quiet and somewhat withdrawn, and starts arguments with comments such as "Why don't you let your feelings show?" Another intense person may prefer a quiet one as a spouse or friend and thus be assured of the place on "center stage."

Threshold of responsiveness refers to the level of stimulation that is needed for a response. Some people are almost insensitive to the sound of noise, the feel of hot or cold weather, the touch of fabrics and other textures. They are not easily bothered at the sensory level. Others may feel very uncomfortable under the same conditions. They may be sensitive to many things, become easily irritated, or experience themselves as having feelings that are easily hurt. Some people are highly responsive to some kinds of stimuli and not to others. For example, their threshold of responsiveness may be high visually and low at an auditory level.

Later in life, persons who are highly aware at the sensory level may have difficulty in crowded or noisy situations. They may express it with "Can't

Temperament Shows in Many Ways

Hebble

Marlis Müller

"Let's tell secrets."

"We never have anything to do."

"Wow, I'm excited!"

"I think I'll
finish this book."

Hebble

you keep those kids quiet?" or "I've got to get away from here for a little peace and quiet."

Quality of mood refers to the amount of friendly, pleasant, and joyful responses a person generally makes. Children with smiling eyes and faces are easier to be around than those who cry and complain. Feeling and acting depressed, they are often depressing to be with. Like climate, the quality of a person's mood often has a strong effect on others.

Persons who are genuinely friendly usually have a strong belief in the basic good of people and are willing to put time and energy into building harmonious relations. They are often popular, for their warmth attracts others.

Distractability is a characteristic parents may like when their children are very little and need to be distracted from potential danger or distracted from a toy that another child "insists" on having. It's a quality parents may dislike as children grow older and are easily distracted from studies or chores. "She's so stubborn" may be said about a child who has low distractability. "He won't pay attention" may be said about a child who is easily distracted. The same comments are often made about grown-ups.

The easily distracted grown-up often has difficulty completing tasks. The phone may ring or someone may drop by and what seemed important one minute before is easily put aside and even forgotten. Such people are often a source of frustration to themselves and to others who prefer closure to a project rather than open-endedness.

Attention span and persistence refers to the length of time a particular activity may be engaged in and the persistence a child shows in doing it in spite of frustration due to lack of skill or interruptions by others. People who are persistent stick with things until finished. They often insist on being heard and keep on asking until they get what they want. People of short attention span and low persistence are often unpredictable because they so often change the focus of their attention.

The persistent grown-up may be quite assertive, either quietly or with a strong voice, yet will continue, for example, with tasks that may require years to complete. If distracted temporarily, such a person will return to the chosen activity and expect to accomplish it, even if it does take a long time.

A Personal Note

When I apply the previous categories to myself, I observe that researching and writing a book such as this has required long persistence and dedication. It has also required me to limit my natural high level of activity and to withdraw often so I could write instead of seeking out new situations which I often prefer.

When concentrating on my writing, I am emotionally irritated by noise and by air pollution. Also my skin is more irritated by certain fabrics and allergic to certain foods than when I am not concentrating so intensely. Furthermore, although I enjoy waking up early and writing at 5:00 A.M. (it's part of my biological rhythm), I miss some evening activities with friends because of going to bed early.

At times I have resented these interferences on my freedom, which of course are self-imposed. After all, no one has "forced" me to write this book except me. When aware of my negative thoughts or feelings, I deliberately change my schedule and allow myself to act in ways that are more in tune with my basic outgoing temperament. Although temperament can be modified and controlled, it feels more "natural" to express it freely, just "as is."

Your Basic Temperament

Consider each of the basic temperament categories. Think of how you were as a child and how you are now, and jot down a few notes to see if there are patterns of breaking free or remaining as is.

Activity level

Rhythm

Approachability

Adaptability

Intensity of reaction

Threshold of responsiveness

Quality of mood

Distractibility

Attention span and persistence

What of the above needs modifying and how could a new inner parent help you?

The Three-Part Personality

Your basic temperament as a child became part of your personality as you grew older. One of the most effective methods for understanding personality is Transactional Analysis (TA). It is based on the theory that each person has three parts to his or her personality: the Parent, the Adult, and the Child. These parts are called ego states. When capitalized, these words will refer to personality; when not, they will refer to people.

When people are in the Parent ego state, they are likely to have opinions similar to those their parent figures once had and to act in similar ways—perhaps critical of muddy shoes or nurturing of skinned knees.

When people are in the Adult ego state, they are processing material in the here and now. They observe, compute, analyze, and make decisions on the basis of facts, not fancy. Being grown up is not the same as being in the Adult ego state. Many grown-ups act like children or parental dictators.

When people are in the Child ego state, they feel and act as they did when they were young—with curiosity and enthusiasm, sadness and withdrawal, anger and rebellion, compliance and hopelessness, and so forth. The younger they are, the more their basic temperament styles are expressed. As people grow up, they often lose their freedom to express themselves naturally and struggle to modify that which is disliked by parent figures.

The TA diagram of personality is represented by three stacked circles: the Parent at the top, the Child at the bottom, and the Adult between the two, often serving as a referee.

Refereeing is frequently necessary because the Parent ego state often "replays" old slogans, injunctions, permissions, and admonitions like a videotape. When the Parent tape is "on," it is heard by the inner Child, who may comply, rebel, procrastinate, or try to ignore the internal messages.

When a person is playing the Parent tape, it is often used on other people who may comply, rebel, procrastinate, or ignore the messages that are given out, verbally or nonverbally.

The Parent ego state begins to develop in early childhood. Children watch their parents or parent figures and start to incorporate their behavior. They may scold their pets, dolls, or younger siblings exactly as they have been scolded themselves.

The Adult ego state also begins its growth in childhood and continues to update the information it has gathered and expand its capacity to process the data until death. Exceptions to this updating occur when illness or accident interferes with the functioning of the brain or when Parent ego-state beliefs or Child ego-state beliefs are so strongly adhered to that new data are rejected. As some people might say, "I've made up my mind; don't confuse me with the facts." The Adult ego state is a powerful part of your personality; with it you can recognize the need for change and do something about it.

The Child ego state emerges at birth, although it is partly programmed as genetic inheritance and the emotional and physical health of the mother inevitably affects the unborn child. As life begins, an infant is concerned only with its physical comfort. Soon, however, it becomes more social, and the first smiles of almost any baby are often greeted with positive acclaim from those around.

Thus the learning process begins and children discover their feelings, which they sometimes turn off. They also discover their bodies and minds, which they may turn on. During the discovery, some children start to rebel, to have temper tantrums, to refuse to obey, and some even run away in order to survive. Others comply. They learn to obey and "be nice" in order to get approval. Still others procrastinate in order to assert their independence.

Personality Shows Through Ego States

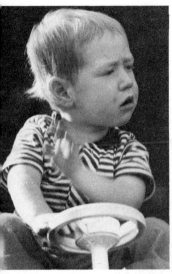

"Stop bothering me."

Jefferey

"How can I figure out what to say?"

Jefferey

Jefferey

"Vrrmmm, here I go!"

Procrastination often starts in response to a parental demand. As children, they are *expected* to say "yes." They often are afraid of saying "no" so they creatively construct a pattern of procrastinating that may last a lifetime. They may procrastinate about applying for a job, going places to make new friends, starting or staying on a diet.

Much of the internal dialogue that goes on inside people's heads is about the expectations between the Parent and Child. At one time in everyone's personal history their parent figures were real live people who could be seen, heard, and touched. Then the parents became incorporated into the Parent ego state. So, too, the Child who was once a real live little boy or girl became covered by the body of a grown-up. Though covered and hidden, the Child remains active, especially when hearing *internal* parent messages, as she or he once heard, or when hearing *external* parent messages. These may come from others on the job or in the home, and the response is often the same as it was in childhood.

Becoming a new good parent to oneself encourages the Child to develop more of its joy of life and creative potentiality. It updates the Adult ego state with new information, new rational thinking skills, and a higher capacity for decision making. It also restructures the Parent ego state in very specific ways.

Learning how to change the Parent part of your personality requires an awareness that some of the characteristics of your historical parents or parent figures were good, and others not so good. Well meaning, perhaps, but not so good. At least, not so good for you.

Not-So-Good Parents

The rationale for developing a new parent and learning to be a good parent to yourself is based on the belief that a new parent can counteract the negative parts of the old. Typical parenting styles that interfere with children's growth toward autonomy include overly critical parents, overly protective parents, inconsistent parents, argumentative parents, uninvolved parents, superorganized parents, and emotionally overly needy parents.

Overly critical parents say such things as, "You're stupid; you'll never amount to anything," or "Can't you ever do anything right?" or "Get lost." When in their Parent ego state, a person who had overly critical parents will use these same words, or imply them with nonverbal ulterior transactions, toward others.

When in their Child ego state, listening to their Parent tapes like a ventriloquist's dummy, they may say things such as, "I don't get it; I guess I'm getting stupid," or "I'm sorry, but I don't understand," or "I'm lost."

Overly protective parents say such things as, "I'll drive you whenever it rains," "Let me do it for you," "Don't worry, I'll take care of everything," "Now you just tell me if those kids are mean to you." When in the Parent ego state, persons who had overly protective parents will act "syrupy" toward other grown-ups, as well as toward children.

When in their Child ego state, they will act overly dependent, always looking for care and protection.

Inconsistent parents say one thing one day and something different the next. On a Tuesday such a parent may say, "I worry about you. You must come home on time," and on Wednesday say, "I don't care what you do; just leave me alone." When in their Parent ego state, persons who have had inconsistent parents will act similarly and vacillate in what they expect from others and may be seen by others as unfair in their demands.

When in their Child ego state, they will feel unsure and frequently check others out, trying to find out what others are thinking or feeling. They look for the nonverbal signs that indicate where the other person is at that particular minute and are not surprised by inconsistency.

Argumentative parents often disagree with each other and with their children about many issues. Their arguments may be loud, even vituperous, or quiet, even rational, or bitter, even cruel, or laughable, even fun. Arguments may arise over work, education, money, leisure time, sex and sex roles, how to rear children, and so forth. Each parent may take an opposing view such as, "Work until you drop dead" versus "Don't work; let someone else support you."

People with argumentative parents often have an inner battle within their Parent ego state. They are likely to act toward others first as one parent did, then as another. They may frequently "go around looking for a fight" as their parents did.

When in the Child ego state, on the other hand, they may feel frightened by loud voices and tend to withdraw when faced with conflict.

Uninvolved parents are those who stay away from home a lot or when home don't listen, or don't share their feelings and ideas, or isolate themselves in a particular room or workshop or activity and say things such as, "Don't bother me, I'm busy," or who act like a proverbial absentminded professor, forgetting birthdays and other special occasions.

When parenting others, people who had uninvolved parents will either act distant, or they will withdraw and be uninvolved as their parents once were.

When in their Child ego state, such people often act friendly but unsure. They may search diligently for someone who will act like an involved parent but at the same time doubt that it could ever happen.

Superorganized parents process data continually; they do not often show childlike warmth and impulsiveness or critical or nurturing parental behavior. People with superorganized parents, when they are in their Parent ego state, are well organized themselves and expect others to be too.

When in their Child ego state, they usually exhibit a pattern of rebellion, indifference, or compliance toward organizations in general and toward organized people in particular.

Emotionally overly needy parents continually expect to be babied and taken care of, or expect to be cheered up and made happy, or expect to be criticized and forgiven. Such parents often manipulate their children into taking parental roles at home. People who have had emotionally overly needy parents will express similar emotional needs or repress them.

When in their Child ego state, they are more likely to act parental, as they were trained to do in childhood. Such people frequently choose a spouse who acts helpless and needs to be taken care of. They also migrate to jobs in which they will take care of others and ignore themselves.

Notes from a Workshop

It was during the third day of a workshop on how to be a good parent to yourself. Some of the participants had entered the workshop knowing what they needed for themselves. Others were not so certain.

Joan was one of these. Quiet, a little withdrawn, responding only when spoken to, she finally blurted out, "I don't know who I am. Sometimes I'm so sure that I'm wife and mother. Other times I'm not at all sure. It all seems empty and half-dead. Of course, being wife and mother is what I *do*, but who am *I*? Actually I'm almost afraid to find out. Maybe I'll discover I'm just an empty shell. I sometimes feel that way. Like a shell on the beach that nothing lives in any more.

"Last night I woke up several times and an old song, I think from a Disney show, was going around in my head. It went, 'I'm nothing but a nothing, a nothing, a nothing. I'm nothing but a nothing. I'm not a thing at all. To be a bat's a dumb thing, a silly and a bum thing. At least a bat is something. I'm not a thing at all.''

With that, Joan's face contorted in pain. Her body contracted. She wrapped her arms around herself and started to rock back and forth as she experienced the terror of feeling like a nothing. Another woman who was sitting beside her gently put her arm around Joan, holding her without talking. The eyes of several people in the room became wet with tears.

One stalwart type of man who usually sat leaning back in a big chair with his arms crossed, leaned forward, uncrossed his arms, looked directly at her, and with admiration proclaimed, "Joan, you've sure got guts and I know what guts are all about. During the war I saw lots of my buddies *doing* something gutsy. Some of them knew why they were doing it. Some didn't. In a strange way you've got just as much guts. You're dealing with the fear that maybe nothing is real, not even you. You didn't have good parents, yet you're trying to be an *ideal* parent when you don't know who you are."

Lisa, a motherly, middle-aged woman interrupted him disapprovingly: "You may call it guts; I call it courage. Now don't ask me to define courage in a situation like this. I don't have it. I just recognize it for what it is, and I think it takes courage for Joan to allow herself to feel who she is and how she got that way. It seems to me that she's breaking through to new awareness. I wish I was free enough to do it."

The Search for Roots

Currently there is a widely expressed interest in discovering historical and biological roots. Often the search for one's roots is generated by a sense of confusion, a feeling of being unable to answer the questions, "Who am I?" and "What am I doing here?"

The two most common forms this interest takes is the study of genealogy with its identification of ancestors and the search for biological parents by people who have been adopted. Although knowing something about ancestors has always been interesting to some people, the popularity of Alex Haley's book *Roots* and its television production accelerated the interest. The personal sense of history was for some a new experience that provided a continuity with the past that felt like a stabilizing force. New awareness of having multiple roots, that is, ethnic, racial, geographical, cultural, has become a tool for breaking free, a key to self-understanding and a new life.

As part of discovering the old life and building a new one, many people have been motivated to search for more personal roots, especially if they have been adopted. Many children wonder about this, feel like outsiders in their own families, feel unloved, or notice their physical appearance is different from their parents'. So they seriously question whether or not the parents who are raising them are *really* their own parents. If told they are adopted, or if they discover this by accident, a common pattern of response emerges. This response includes trying very hard to please their adoptive parents, repressing negative thoughts about them, being angry at their biological parents, and wondering how things might be different if they had lived with them instead of with their adoptive ones.

In some situations adults are allowed to examine legal records in the search for their biological parents. In other situations they cannot: "the case is closed." The closed case, with the many unanswered questions, may perpetuate a person's confusion about his or her identity.

However, even people who know their roots may also know confusion if *forced* into uprootedness. Forced uprootedness is experienced by people who must flee from their homelands during the terrors of war, plague, or poverty. When they arrive in another country where language or customs are different and their friends and family may be nonexistent, the sense of being alone, without cultural roots, can be overpowering. Free, perhaps, from the terrors of their own country, they may at the same time feel like motherless children. Many children whose ties with close friends and schools are broken when their family moves or when their parents are divorced also feel uprooted and uncertain.

Thus, the temperament styles people have inherited, the personalities they have developed, the restrictive or permissive situations under which they

Something's Missing. It's not the Same.

Hebble

Hebble

"Never to return?"

"It has such an
empty feeling."

"What will happen to us now?"

live, are all intertwined. The resulting patterns may contribute to a sense of rootlessness or to a sense of being uprooted or to a sense of roots. Yet even people with a sense of roots may or may not feel free. In most cases they need to reparent themselves somewhat so that they can design a new life that leads to joy, even to happiness.

Breakthrough II—Personality Styles of Parents

The purpose of these breakthrough exercises is to increase your awareness of parenting styles and what you, in particular, need to become a good parent to yourself.

Your Use of Ego States: At various times most people switch their energy from one ego state to another. Within a moment a person's posture, tone of voice, words, and facial expressions may shift. For example, a person having a childlike temper tantrum may suddenly change and act like a critical parent.

For this exercise, think of several situations where somebody said or did something unexpected.

What was your initial response? What did you do next?

Were your responses similar to the ones your parent or parent figures would have made?

If so, is there any change needed so you can get on with a new life?

Typical Negative Parenting: All parents are unique in the details of how they parent. Yet there may be some general negative parenting styles that your parents used. Fill in the following columns where appropriate.

Negative Parenting Styles	How Did the Style Show?	How Did You Respond?
Overcritical		
Overprotective		
Inconsistent		
Argumentative		
Uninvolved		
Superorganized		
Emotionally overneedy		

Typical Positive Parenting: The positive parenting styles listed below are the *opposite* of those in the previous exercise. Fill in the columns where appropriate.

Positive Parenting Styles	How Did It Show?	How Did You Respond?
Reasonable		
Encouraging		
Consistent		
Mediating		
Caring		
Relaxed		
Responsible		

Which words most describe each of the parent figures you had when you were young?

Journal Record: Some people keep diaries or journals hoping others will see what's inside. Record your insights in your journal, but let this be primarily for you. After you have finished, go back and put the letters "P," "A," or "C" beside each paragraph that seems to be written from the orientation of one of your ego states.

Spellbound
or Free

3

From witches and warlocks
and ghoulies and ghoasties
and long-leggedy beasties
and things that go bump in the night—
Good Lord, deliver us.

   Old Scottish Prayer

Freedom is not a destination. It is a continuing journey. Carlos Castanedas wrote, "Does this path have a heart? If it does, the path is good; if it doesn't, it is of no use." The freedom road is a lifelong challenge. The road seems to be straight and smooth; then suddenly a bump, a rut, a sharp corner, even a collapse of the road itself appears. The road that seemed so sure and safe changes; so does the direction of one's life. One issue is solved, another emerges. The background becomes the foreground.

This chapter focuses on the "dumb and ugly" spells that are cast on children when parents and culture continually send them negative messages. These messages interfere with the power of breaking free. In this chapter you will learn to identify spells in general and specific spells that were cast over you because of parental injunctions and cultural values.

Parents as Witches and Warlocks

Because of feeling spellbound, many people have a difficult time breaking through to the reality of freedom. They lack a sense of power and autonomy; they defeat themselves with negative ideas they picked up in childhood and have carried throughout their lives. They are spellbound.

The belief in spells is as old as time. So are the feelings of awe and fear when faced with spellbinders or magicians—either men or women.

Since the dark ages, women have been called witches and their male counterparts called warlocks. Witches were spellbinders, and fairy tales are full of both good and bad witches. Warlocks were supposed to be demons who broke their promises. The word comes from Old English words meaning "oath breaker."

Many children regard their parents as though they were witches and warlocks. A common accusation a rebellious child uses against a mother is, "You're an old witch." The word *warlock* is less commonly known, yet the idea of being a demon who breaks promises is implied in a resentful remark of a child to a father, "You always say you're going to take me somewhere for fun, but you never keep your word."

When parents act like witches or warlocks, breaking their promises day after day, most children lose their sense of trust. Without trust they may feel adrift like a rowboat at sea, or feel like a caged hamster on a wheel, going around and around and not getting anywhere, or feel like someone almost buried by a landslide and unable to move.

Notes from a Workshop

As a child, Catherine was spellbound with her fantasies of ghosts. She had grown up in a big old house in the country. Her parents had been killed in an accident, so she lived with her elderly, pious grandparents. They gave her the message that life was serious. "You never know," they said; "death is always waiting for you just around the corner."

Catherine described her feelings. "The days were lonely, but the nights were terrible. I would be in bed in that big old creaky house, and I was so scared that sometimes I couldn't move. I'd just shiver with fear. Sometimes I used to pray a funny old prayer instead of the one my grandparents said I should use. My prayer was like this: 'From ghoulies and ghosties and long-legged beasties, and things that go bump in the night, dear Lord deliver me.' I would say it over and over and really work myself up. It sounds silly now, but when the wind whistled through the trees and the old wood on the steps creaked and groaned and sounded like someone in pain, the prayer gave me comfort. I didn't feel so trapped and spellbound. Then I would look at an old photo of my mom and dad and get down under the blankets and just cry.

"Now I'm thirty-three years old and I still hate to be alone, especially on stormy nights. I almost feel like I could go crazy with fear, and neither my parents nor grandparents nor anyone else could save me."

The Magic of Spells

Everybody is spellbound in one way or another, with or without awareness. The spells may be positive, negative, or so-so. The most tragic spells cast by parents or substitute parents are spells that interfere with autonomy and freedom. Less destructive are those that give a biased or inadequate view of reality. Positive spells, on the other hand, affirm the person in ways that contribute to the search for freedom.

A spell is a compelling incantation, word, or formula that seems to have magic qualities. "Don't you dare ever go out of the back yard" may cast a spell that restricts the desire for exploration. "If you ask one more time, I'll give you a beating you won't ever forget" may cast a spell that restricts the desire to ask for things.

Other parental spells may not appear to be negative, yet they are. If said frequently, "I know you can do it if you *just try harder*" becomes a spell. It does not allow for possible failure, only for achievement. "Everything's going to turn out all right" is another potential spell. If it is heard often enough, children may not learn how to put out the energy that is necessary to solve problems. In fact, they may go through life wearing rose-colored glasses, expecting a magician to make everything all right.

In a more positive vein, spells may also be woven by parents who say, "I'm glad you work hard," "You always show lots of courage," "You're great at solving problems." Each of these parental assessments is powerful. The parental approval of a child's being and doing is a healthy spell with a magical quality.

Magic is something that appeals to most children. The thought of it may send shivers of fear or anticipation up and down their spines. The most powerful magicians to children are often their parents who seem to use supernatural powers.

Spells Lead to Confusion

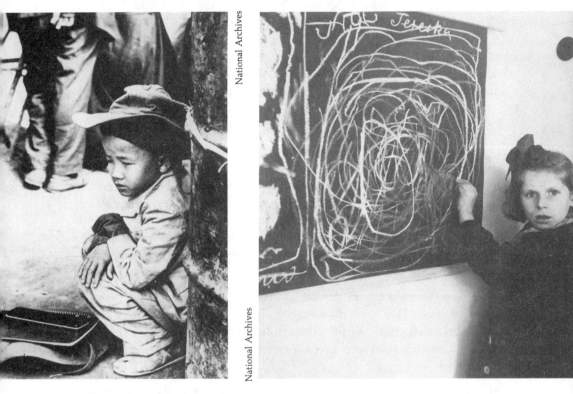

National Archives

National Archives

"I'm so worried
I can't think."

"I don't know who I am!"

"I don't understand."

National Archives

The belief in magic spells doesn't go away as people get older. Although grown-ups may say they don't believe in magic, it's not uncommon to hear them say:

"I'm scared even if there's nothing to be afraid of."

"I'm caught in a web of my own making."

"I always knew I was born to lose."

"My crazy life . . . "

It's not uncommon for people to carry a talisman for protection, or to avoid black cats or walking under ladders or stepping on a crack. "Bad luck comes in threes," one might say. "My luck is running high tonight," says another. Each statement or behavior points to the belief in magic and the power of spells.

Recognizing Spells

When you were a child, you probably decided, "That's the way I am and that's the way I'll always be." This decision was like a spell with magic power. Who cast it?

What spells did you hear about? Where you could go? Who to play with? How smart you were? How pretty/handsome you were? What you would be when you grew up?

Based on these spells, what were some of the decisions you made as a child about *who you are as a person?*

What are some of the decisions you made about *what you could do?*

In what ways are you still bound or free from these childhood spells?

The Process of Spellbinding

People become spellbound by being brainwashed, hypnotized, or conditioned by parent figures and culture.

In breaking through to freedom, a brainwashed person can be reprogrammed; negative hypnotic suggestions can be discarded; conditioning can be overruled and changed. Spells are broken if they are recognized as such.

When the word *brainwashed* is used, political dissidents, war criminals, and cult followers are the people who most often come to mind. People who are brainwashed are systematically deprived of what their bodies need, subjected to fearful treatment that undermines their sense of identity, and programmed to believe in the propaganda of their captors. They are often isolated from others so that they lose their sense of belongingness and are stripped of personal possessions, which often are symbols of self-esteem.

Many parents use deprivation and fear to brainwash and spellbind their children:

> "I'll beat you within an inch of your life if you don't behave!"
>
> "Just wait till I get that switch on you!"
>
> "You won't get a thing to eat tonight!"
>
> "Crybaby! I'll give you something to cry for!"
>
> "Don't you dare talk back!"

Being *hypnotized* is different than being brainwashed. When people are brainwashed, they have no choice; when hypnotized, they have a choice. They can agree or disagree with the hypnotist and allow themselves to be hypnotized or not. In the hands of someone who is ethical and well trained, hypnosis can be a valuable tool for understanding and change. In the hands of someone who is not, it can be used to take advantage of those who are weaker.

One of the most powerful influences today that functions much like a popular hypnotist is the TV. Many people choose to go along with it, to agree with the mumbo-jumbo of the visual and audio stimulation. "That's the way the world is," they conclude. Freedom is often presented in cops-and-robbers chases rather than as internal growth. Joy is represented by gyrating bodies or solutions to corny soap operas. The sportscasters and the Saturday-Sunday-Monday football games are hypnotic to sports enthusiasts.

Parents may start the hypnotic process with instructions such as, "Look at me while I talk to you." Then, when a child's attention is focused, a parent may try to make a "hypnotic" suggestion such as, "You can do anything if you just work hard enough."

Occasionally children are able to "hypnotize" their parents. Usually, however, it is the parents who take the role of the hypnotist and may succeed or not. A child who hears words such as, "You're a stupid kid," "You're a stupid kid," You're a stupid kid," may agree or disagree.

The spell is cast if the child agrees with the hypnotist. Then the words "I'm stupid" are endlessly repeated in his or her mind. If a child disagrees, then the parents may be considered stupid and a spell is not cast.

In spite of how often parents say "Do this" or "Do that," if the children doubt the importance of parental commands, they freely think what they like. They are not spellbound, they are free—at least in their minds.

Being *conditioned* is different from being brainwashed or hypnotized. Being conditioned is being trained to respond to specific stimuli in specific ways. It uses a continuous educational reward-punishment process to modify a person's natural or learned behavior. The "oughts" and "musts" of family and society become internalized, including beliefs that certain things are true when in fact they may not be. Habits and manners are usually the results of conditioning. Sometimes they become compulsive.

Freedom is rare. "I absolutely must always have the dishes clean" is a statement from a person who has been conditioned to be a "cleaner-upper" and has become compulsive about it. This person actually believes that certain tasks "absolutely" "must" "always" be done, although there are no data to support the belief.

"I just can't . . . [get up early, go to bed early, etc.]" also points to feeling compulsive—enslaved because of a spell.

Notes From a Workshop

Sarah was a slave to her house. She was married and had no children. Yet each day she would rise early and completely clean the house so it was always immaculate. Each evening she would repeat the ritual for a total of six hours a day, every day, even on holidays.

The Spell of Routine

"When I grow up. . . ."

"Do it now!"

"Men first."

Between cleaning chores, she cooked. Simple cooking was not enough. Each dish of every meal was a gourmet's delight. She deliberately chose difficult, time-consuming recipes and seldom took time to sit down and visit with friends and relatives. In fact she had few friends, only acquaintances whom she would try to impress with her house and food.

Her husband found their dog to be better company and had little to say to her except, angrily, "Stop pushing food at me all the time. I don't want so much." Yet Sarah continued her compulsive behavior.

In medieval times to be compulsive was to be labeled as "possessed by demons." Compulsive people don't do what they *want* to do but what they feel *driven* to do because of essentially unconscious conditioning factors.

They need to do self-reparenting by giving themselves "permission" to relax, to be less than perfect, to be enjoyed by others, not only for accomplishments but for being whom they are.

They need to reparent themselves because the compulsions and spells they live by may have little to do with reality and a lot to do with imagination, fantasy, and a story-book view of life.

Waiting for a Spellbreaker

Some people go through life expecting someone to come along who will break the negative spells they are under. They do not see themselves as having the potential to be a good witch or a good wizard with the power to break spells.

Remember when you were young. Who or what did you wait for?

What did you hope would happen?

How did it turn out?

The Dumb and Ugly Club

Faced with spellbinding negative messages, many children give in to them. When they do, they often, knowingly or unknowingly, join the Dumb and Ugly Club.

This club is a worldwide organization that anyone may join. There is no discrimination on the basis of race, religion, ethnic background, sex, or age. The only membership requirement is commitment to a negative personal self-image.

The names of the charter members are lost in history, though many well-known people over the centuries have belonged. Most people join the club during their childhood years—often to be part of the gang—yet it is possible to join at any time in one's life.

Furthermore, with a deep commitment to being dumb and ugly, it is possible to earn "advanced" membership. Advanced members often have the chance to chair Dumb-and-Ugly regional meetings where members are encouraged to complain about how dumb and ugly they are.

I used to belong to this club. I equated beauty as being like my mother—tall, blonde, and with long, straight hair, whereas I am a brunette with curly hair and of medium height. I also used to qualify as a dumb member. Although I did not get that message from my family or teachers and in fact always got top grades, I think I concluded I was dumb because I didn't know how to fix my hair. Also there were some things I did not understand because my parents seldom discussed anything of a personal nature with me. So when something unexpected happened, like their divorce, I felt confused and dumb because I hadn't seen it coming.

What happened to me in school also contributed to my self-image. From the fourth to the sixth grades, I was in a small experimental group for so-called bright kids. We were allowed to do anything we wanted—go to classes or organize our own time individually or in a group. The only requirement was that we be in the school building during the school hours. I did not like my math or spelling teachers so did not go to those classes. Consequently I am very poor at basic math—times tables, percentages, decimal points, and similar skills learned in those grades are not mine. Even as simple an arithmetic problem as figuring my book royalties usually turns out wrong. You may laugh because you didn't belong to the Dumb and Ugly Club. As for me, when I try to figure my potential income, not knowing what to do with all the zeros and the decimal points, the results of my dumb figuring are often way off base.

As for spelling, simple words such as *address* or *fence* that most people commonly spell correctly without thinking, may require thinking on my part because they are not programmed into my inner Child. "Is it one *d* or two, one *s* or two in 'address,' or is it *s* or *c* in fence?" My manuscripts have many little markings after fifth-grade and sixth-grade words. These markings are a clue to my secretary that I am not sure of the spelling so she should please check carefully. For some unknown reason, seventh-grade words are not so hard for me and, when in doubt, I can even find them in a dictionary.

When I entered the university at age thirty-five and took the entrance exams, I thought very carefully about the simple kinds of words and avoided using them unless I was sure I was spelling them right. After all, I didn't want to take a non-unit course known as "bonehead English." It would take time and, for me, be embarrassing to be labeled a bonehead, meaning dumb. I often wish I had taken the course. It might be easier for me to write now.

As for math, now that computers are so much a part of daily life, it may not be necessary to know the basics. However, the spell is still on me. When I was growing up, a million years ago (see, I told you I didn't know math), girls were not expected to understand or use machinery and, to the little girl inside of me, computers are very complicated machinery. So too, if there is a knock in the engine of my car or if it performs in a different way, a part of me becomes unduly concerned. "I don't understand," I may say to myself. "Something terrible may happen." The car could blow up just as my life seemed to with my parents' divorce and the breakdown of our family unit.

As for feeling ugly, I guess I concluded that when I was a little girl, when I compared myself to others. I used to stand in front of the mirror and say to myself, "You're ugly, ugly, ugly." When in my teens I had learned the colors and styles that were attractive on me, my brother would often tease me with, "Beauty is only skin deep and you've been skinned."

My father was a professor of dentistry, but my teeth were not pretty. He said they were too soft for bands, so for about a year when I was ten years old, each morning he would have me sit on the side of my bed and push on my teeth to improve the alignment. That worked then; however, in the last few years they have once more gotten out of alignment. I don't like it and have suggested to dentists that they pull them out and give me beautiful replacements like movie stars have. They are always so horrified at the idea that I drop the subject. Yet the doubt remains in my head: Who is right, the dentist or my inner Child?

I regret to say it has taken me many years to break out of these spells. Having strong opinions about who I am and the meaning of what I do, I had to get in touch with my yearning for freedom before I was willing to give up my self-label of being dumb. It took even more to give up my self-image of being ugly. That happened only about five years ago.

I was leading a workshop where three women during a lunch break were complaining about their appearance. As I listened, I said to myself, "Do I sound like that?" The answer was, "Yes, I do," so I immediately *decided* I could learn to fix my own hair; that I wasn't dumb and that I didn't need to feel ugly any more. Don't misunderstand me. I don't think I'm beautiful. Beauty is in the eyes of the beholder and "some of my very best friends have dark hair." Although I still admire women who look like my mother looked when I was little, I now believe I'm attractive and I enjoy that belief.

Parental Spellbinding Injunctions

All children receive messages or injunctions about their worth from their parents. These messages contribute to a child's sense of positive self-esteem and/or to the sense of low, negative esteem. A child who receives only positive messages will have much less need for self-reparenting than will those who have the opposite, negative experience. However, even if a child has ideal parents, there are often other significant persons, such as teachers, stepparents, grandparents, or older siblings, who give injunctions that interfere with the child's health and happiness.

Injunctions are commands, directives, or orders. The word is used here to refer to statements or acts by parenting figures that adversely affect children's sense of being alive and well, capable and competent, free and joyful. Injunctions, like spells, may lead to lifelong problems with or without the awareness of those who give them or those who receive them. Depending upon how they are given, the injunctions may brainwash, hypnotize, or condition a child.

There are a number of basic negative injunctions, according to psychotherapists Mary and Robert Goulding. The first two are against *being* itself. They

Some Parents Encourage Freedom

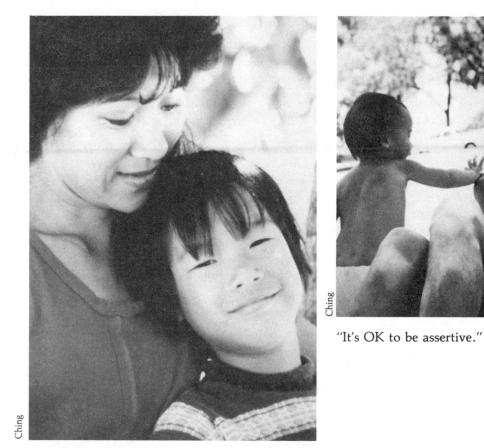

Ching

"It's OK to be close."

Ching

"It's OK to be assertive."

"It's OK to get attention."

James

are "Don't be . . . " and "Don't be you." Two are about relationships: "Don't be close" and "Don't belong." Next are those concerned with personal growth: "Don't grow up" and "Don't be a child." Others are against physical or emotional wellness: "Don't be well" and "Don't be sane." Two are against achievement: "Don't be important" and "Don't succeed."

Don't Be: This is a lethal injunction, a message that is given by parents who do not want a particular child to exist.

The parents may not be married and may not know, or want to know, how to cope with the problems involved. Or they may already have "too many children" and not want "one more mouth to feed" or "one more diaper to change" because they are physically or economically drained, with no relief in sight. Or they may dislike each other and see a child as a burden that might be a pressure to keep them together.

Now with the wide use of birth control, parents may have a timetable for when they want a child. Yet if it comes at the "wrong time" when job or college or other issues are more important, a child may get a "Don't be" message.

Don't Be You: Although not as lethal as "Don't be," this message also hits at the basic sense of self. It is most strongly given by parents who want a child to be of the opposite sex than the one who is born. They may give this child a name that reflects their wishes and train the child in ways that strongly interfere with the development of self-esteem and comfort and satisfaction with one's body.

Don't Be Close: This negative injunction is often given by parents who see themselves as "too busy" to listen to, comfort, play with, or teach a child. They may give out a message such as "Leave me alone" or "Stay out of my way" or "Don't bother me." This injunction is also given by parents who abandon their children. A child who is abandoned may decide not to love ever again or not ever to be close to a person of the same sex as the parent who left. A child may make a similar decision if a parent dies. Death feels like abandonment.

Another way this injunction is experienced is when divorce, or continuing conflict, splinters a family. When strong bitterness is expressed between parents, they may compete for the affection of a child and issue the message, "Don't be close to that so-and-so of an ex-spouse; only be close to me."

Don't Belong: Children experience this injunction if they are rejected by parents who wish a particular child were not part of the family—often because of some problem a child has. In such cases, it is not unusual for children to fantasize being adopted. They may have previously received messages of "Don't be" or "Don't be you" or "Don't belong to us" from their parents, so they feel as if they don't quite belong. Adopted children may feel the same, or more so.

Some children are taught that they are either better than others or not as good as others; thus they may also feel like outsiders. So, too, if they are rejected by their peers or by their teachers, they can experience a "You don't belong" message.

The above four injunctions sometimes are interrelated. For example, when people do not feel as if they belong, they may give up hope of ever getting close to others. They may also feel as if they're wrong in being who they are and perhaps that they shouldn't have been born at all.

Don't Grow Up: This is the command of parents who want their children to remain dependent and under their control. In spite of what they say, they do not want children to grow up or to think or act independently. They want obedience and compliance to their opinions, ideas, and dictates. By keeping their child or children dependent, these parents are assured of a lifetime of worrying. This may increase their false sense of importance. Many parents seem to fall apart when the last child leaves home. These parents may be very critical or very nurturing or both. The fact is, they have an overly abundant need to be needed.

Don't Be a Child: This injunction is just the opposite of "Don't grow up." The "Don't be a child" message often includes "Don't feel." It is often given by parents who themselves act like children. They reverse the parent-child roles and insist that their children care for them—either physically or psychologically—rather than in the more appropriate way.

"Don't be a child" may also be given by parents who are overly ambitious for their children and who want them to be geniuses, whether they are or not. Pushing their children to compete and be first, such parents often feel academically inadequate and use their children as compensation for what they miss in themselves.

The same message often accompanies a "Don't be close" injunction given by parents who are too busy and refuse to listen to what they may label as "kid stuff" or "childish concerns." The same message comes through if they continually refuse to play with their children or imply that play is less important than work.

Don't Be Well: This is another injunction given by parents with the need to be needed and the need to keep children dependent. After all, if a child is not well, then a parent's attention is required, which may lead the parent into feeling important. In some cases the parent may choose to feel like a martyr so as to receive sympathy from others for having an unhealthy child. In some cases "Don't be well" is a disguise for the lethal "Don't be." An emotionally sick parent may feel stuck with an unwanted child and hope the child might die if he or she is sick enough.

Don't Be Sane: An injunction to be crazy may be given by parents who do not want their children to be sane because they might see how crazy their parents are. It is also given with remarks such as "You're impossible; you act so crazy," "Can't you think like a rational human being?!" "There must be something wrong with your mind!" "Don't be sane" is often related to "Don't grow up" (because if you do grow up you might think).

Don't Succeed: Like parents who want others to remain dependent on them, some parents do not want their children to have more success than they have themselves. Their reasoning might go, "He'll get conceited and will avoid us," or "She'll get so successful she'll be too busy for us [or move away or judge us negatively, and so forth]."

Such parents might give the injunction by continually criticizing less than perfect grades so that a child concludes, "I'm not perfect; therefore I can't succeed." When grown up these persons may almost reach their goals, then do something at the last minute that undermines their achievements.

Don't Be Important: To be important is to be special and to be recognized as such. Children with a "Don't be" or "Don't be you" injunction also believe they are not important as individuals. Their parents may pay more attention to a more favored child, or to a job, or a hobby, and use comments such as "Don't bother me" or "Don't be such a nuisance" or "Don't be a show-off; you're no better than anyone else." They structure their time and interactions in such a way that their children conclude, "My needs are not important; therefore I'm not important."

Don't . . . : This more generalized injunction is like a spell that seemingly paralyzes the person who receives it. It is given with comments such as, "Don't go out of your backyard, something terrible might happen" or "Don't contradict me or something terrible will happen."

People who receive this injunction are continually fearful of an assertive position, of sticking up for themselves, of making decisions, of doing something new, of thinking, of changing, of taking charge of their own lives.

Sometimes injunctions are imagined by children and are not actually given by their parents or by the environment. That's not the point now, though it will be later. The point now is that when people believe an injunction is true, it becomes part of their self-image and interferes with the feeling of being fully alive and well.

In the struggle to fight against negative injunctions, it takes great courage for a child to say, "Don't say 'don't' to me so much." It takes even more courage to decide to exist, to *be:* "I will *be* and I will *be me* in spite of people who did not want me or who did not want me to be myself."

It also takes courage to decide to *do:* "I will think clearly, I will achieve many of my goals, I will love and trust and be close to people, I will be *alive* and *well.*"

The courage to be and the courage to do are universal human qualities. Everyone has them and uses them or has them and has not yet recognized and developed this part of themselves that leads down the road to freedom.

Recognizing Injunctions

Study the list of negative injunctions you personally experienced in the process of growing up. Then number them from 1 to 10 according to their effect on you. Number 1 would be the one that seems most pervading in your life.

Now, opposite each negative injunction, make up a positive one that would contradict it. Remember, an injunction is like a command. So start your sentences with "You can" or with "Do."

Negative Injunctions   *Positive Injunctions*

Don't be

Don't be you

Don't be close

Don't belong

Don't grow up

Don't be a child

Don't be well

Don't be sane

Don't succeed

Don't be important

Start now to use these new positive injunctions as a way of being a good parent to yourself. You can write them on 3" × 5" cards and carry them in your pocket. You can write them on a mirror where you will see them often or on a sheet of paper taped to the refrigerator door. Or put them on a cassette tape and play the tape frequently, especially when you wake up and just before you go to sleep.

Spells of the Cultural Parent

Many spells under which people live are due to their various cultures, which function in many ways like a parent. Each person incorporates a "cultural parent" in addition to his or her historical parents.

The cultural parent includes the national culture and the many subcultures with their various social, ethnic, geographic, economic, and religious sub-groupings. Even a peer subculture often has parental control and spellbinding effects.

Some cultures consciously spellbind children of certain groups that they are one way or the other—dumb and ugly or fortunate and beautiful. Other cultures do it less consciously yet with equal effectiveness.

The cultural parent is comprised of the collective beliefs a group holds, whether these beliefs are conscious or unconscious. When they are unconscious, they make up what can be called the spirit of the culture. When the beliefs are conscious, they become the mores, laws, and regulations that people are "supposed" to live by. They are beliefs that are taught, and often thought, to be true. They often become spells. The tragedy of the mass suicide at Guyana shows the spell a subculture may cast on its members.

The march toward freedom requires an awareness of how a culture acts as a parent and then an awareness of what the spirit of the culture is and how the spirit affects people. When educational institutions or consciousness-raising groups take on change-agent functions, they often help people become conscious of the cultural parent and at the same time may help shift its focus, decrease or increase its importance.

This occurred, for example, during the 1960s when the collective cultural parent of black people made major changes in itself. As a result, instead of listening to the many negative social messages about themselves, blacks began to respond to new leaders who were change agents proclaiming, "Black is beautiful" and "I'm black and proud." This rediscovery of the spirit was accompanied by a new awareness of what it means to be "soul brothers" and "soul sisters" on the freedom road.

Within the spirit of any cultural parent are many myths and images. For example, one of the widely accepted cultural myths in the United States is that a poor man can become president, although it has never happened. Another is that a woman would not make a good president, although that has never happened—yet!

The cultural parent also contains generalized ideas about issues such as what is considered right and wrong in a particular culture: "Children should be . . . ," "Women should be . . . ," "Men should be . . . ," "People of various racial, ethnic, and religious backgrounds should be . . . ," and so forth.

Each culture may have a brainwashing, hypnotizing, or conditioning effect on those who are part of it. In the theory of Transactional Analysis, this is called "cultural scripting." As with a theatrical script, people may decide to play the expected roles or may refuse to do so. Each culture and subculture has its own dramatic patterns, its entrances and exits, its characters, dialogues, and script themes.

A common script theme in U.S. culture is the work-hard script. Inherited from those who first came to this country to exploit it or to escape persecution, the work-hard script was acted out by people who were pioneers and/or settlers. This is still a strong cultural script, although many people are seeing it as a spell and are "working hard" to break free from it.

Prolonged financial support of young adults as though they were children and the availability of government financial aid encourages some people to

Expectations and Culture

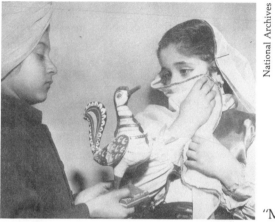

National Archives

"May I give you a gift?"

National Archives

Rapho/Photo Researchers

"How are we different, and how the same?"

"Blessed be the Lord. . . ."

"Subcultures have their own expectations."

Moon/Stock, Boston, Inc.

avoid working and thus break the spell of the script. Furthermore, many people are resisting the work-hard demand and instead are demanding "more money for less work" or "more play instead of work." These are new so-called freedom slogans that emerge in affluent cultures where survival needs are widely, though not totally, met. However, the current swing to postpone retirement points to a return to a "working hard" script.

Spells of the cultural parent are often transmitted through the historical parents or substitute parents by use of stories. Legends, fairy tales, myths, and adventure fantasies all have the power of spellbinding children in ways that may interfere with freedom in later life. These stories may be told, read, or observed on television. The current popularity of superheroes is perpetuating a cultural parent—to be "super." People who do not choose to go along with this expectation may be seen by others as spellbound.

Cultural Spells

Think of spells you believe you are under because of a cultural or sub-cultural script you live by. Then fill in the following:

One of my cultural scripts or spells is _____

The myth, legend, or story that goes with it is _____

_____.

Character types and the roles they are supposed to play are _____

_____.

The role that I most often identify with is _____.

Strengths of this cultural script are _____.

Weaknesses of this cultural script are _____

_____.

To become free of this, I need to develop an inner parent who would

_____.

A Personal Note

One of the cultural stories that spellbound me was from Aesop's fables. I often read it when I was young. The story was about a very young shepherd whose task was to tend sheep in the mountains. Sometimes this child would call out to the village that a wolf was coming to attack the sheep, when actually it wasn't. When the young shepherd called, the villagers would run to help. Then one day the wolf did come but the villagers did not. They had been called so many times they no longer believed in the potential danger.

This was a potent story for me. What I learned from it was:

> Learn to tell the difference between real and imagined danger.
>
> Don't pretend to others that there is danger when there isn't.
>
> Do not ask for help and protection unless danger surely exists.
>
> Even if danger does exist, help may not come. Therefore learn how to take care of yourself even if you are afraid.

I have not reread that story since my childhood, and what I remember of it may not be the way it was written. Even today I am still somewhat under that spell. Whether it is OK or not, I seldom feel free to ask for help. I feel as if asking is a bother to other people. I think I got the childhood message from my parents, "Don't bother us."

I also think this Aesop's fable fits into a spell or script that was cast both by my culture and by my family—pioneering in search of freedom. A pioneering script calls for people to be strong and independent, doing it on their own, seldom asking for help, and I am usually like this.

Nevertheless a part of me still feels unsafe. Perhaps it is because my father was sometimes so mean to my older brother for not getting good grades in Latin in school. No one rescued my brother when he cried for "help," and I was afraid for him and afraid I would be next.

Now as a therapist, I understand irrational anger irrationally expressed and can help a client work it through. I believe irrational anger is a sign of slavery, not freedom. Also when people fantasize danger that doesn't exist, I wish they wouldn't, but I can understand their fears. I know that one of the reasons I married my husband is because my Child was wise enough to say intuitively "Yes" to a man who is both nurturing and protective of me from both real or imagined wolves.

Breakthrough III—Diagnosing Your Own Parents

The purpose of this Breakthrough is to help you get a clearer perspective of your own parent figures. You will be looking for both their positive and negative traits *as they were when you were young.*

Attributes of your parents: On the form that follows, use one column for your mother, another for your father, another for other parent figures if you had them.

List each parent's positive attributes—their words, their actions, their values, and so forth. This is important because when you are unhappy, your parents' positive attributes can give you strength if you keep them in your awareness. They are part of you whether you know it or not or whether you allow yourself to use these qualities or not.

Next record their negative spellbinding attributes—their words, actions, and values—that interfered with their own lives or with yours.

If one of your parents was not there in your childhood, it was probably a negative experience. You may have interpreted that parent as disinterested.

If you grew up in an institution of some kind, it may have functioned as both mother and father in a critical or caring way.

If you had a stepparent or older sibling when you were young, those persons may have functioned as parents to you and be part of your parent ego state.

Mother's Attributes		*Father's Attributes*		*Attributes of Other Parent Figures*	
+	−	+	−	+	−

Positives and negatives in your parent ego state

Subdivide the two large circles below with vertical lines. Jot down the characteristics of each person in each section.

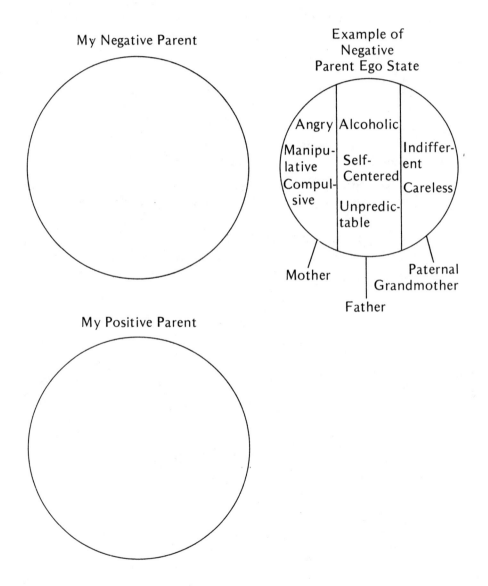

My Negative Parent

Example of
Negative
Parent Ego State

My Positive Parent

Study these two circles and reflect on your spellboundness.

Owning your parents

Many characteristics of the parents and parent figures you once had were incorporated into your personality and became your Parent ego state. Which ones do you own up to? Which have you rejected?

Positive characteristics of my parents that I sometimes use.	*Situations in which I use them.*
Negative characteristics of my parents that I sometimes use.	*Situations in which I use them.*
Characteristics of my parents that I rejected and do not use.	*How and when I made this decision to be different.*

In your journal, record your insights of how each of these other parenting figures affected your sense of who you are and your acceptance or rejection of what you do.

Adapting
to Authority

4

Children aren't happy with nothing to ignore and that's
what parents are created for.
   Ogden Nash

Parents do not like to be ignored. If they are ignored, they may become very angry and shout their instructions even more loudly: "Get your tail over here!" "Knock that off or I'll knock it off for you." They may act sad and manipulative: "You don't love me, your poor old father, any more." They may become threatening: "If you do that again, I'll leave you at the orphanage." They may become indifferent: "You don't pay any attention to me so I don't care anymore." Some parents try harder in nurturing ways to be understood and heard.

This chapter will describe the impact of parental authority on children and various ways they choose to adapt, the most common being obedience, rebellion, and procrastination. You will have an opportunity to increase your personal awareness in order to change your style of adapting, especially to authority.

Parent Power

Obedience to authority, widely praised by parents, teachers, and society as a whole, is first learned in the home. Necessary? Yes. And yet . . .

From the time of birth, children are taught rules and regulations and are taught to obey them. Some are life-enhancing. Some are not. When using parent power, first comes the content—the rules of the injunction. Then comes the command to obey—the power of the injunction. Directives such as "Do as I say" are power plays. The implication is, "If you do as I say, you'll be rewarded positively and if you don't, you'll suffer the consequences of disobedience."

Many parents believe that one of their primary tasks is training their children to obey. The training may be brutal and may destroy a child's sense of selfhood. It may be loving and increase a child's sense of self-esteem. It may fluctuate at different times, for different reasons, around different subjects.

Whatever the methods, parents usually justify their actions. They are "only doing their duty" as parents. And all too often they interpret their duty as the need to develop compliant, obedient children—in other words, "good" children who will not argue back, think independently, or rebel against their dictates.

In *parent-team families* where two parents act as a team—either negatively or positively—children find out that they can't play off one against the other. The power base is strong and predictable. Sometimes, as a team with specific assignments, one parent may "power" the children's homework and the other may "power" getting the chores done. Children adapt very quickly to the parent team and to the ways the parents express their power. When the expression is positive, children feel safe; when negative, they feel overwhelmed and as if there is no way out.

In *uneven parent-power families* one parent has the power; the other is relatively powerless. Often the powerful one has a self-righteous position and believes that he or she is right. In some families one parent is so weak that the other feels it is essential to be strong. It is not unusual for a person who feels hopeless and without power to say something like, "I give up. You do it. It's up to you to decide." Children adapt by playing one parent against the other. They often act in ways to get the two parents to fight. As grown-ups, they are likely to replay the same scenario or avoid persons like their parents.

In *single-parent families* the power base may be held by the parent or by one or more children who control the parent. When held by the parent, the power can be expressed as loving and open and encouraging of growth; or controlling, closed, and discouraging of growth; or fluctuating between both. When the power is held by the children, anarchy often reigns.

In *divorced families* where the children spend some time with each parent, there is often conflict around who's really in charge. "You tell your father *I'll* decide what kind of shoes you need." "You tell your mother *I'll* decide what time I'll get you home." Some children are able to adapt to conflict between divorced parents and to different standards and uses of power as they go from parent to parent, stepparent to stepparent. Others become overly compliant, or defiant and rebellious, or indifferent. The use and abuse of parent power may become an issue to them as they see themselves as pawns with little power to direct their own lives.

In *group families* several families choose to live together. Currently there is a significant increase in group-living arrangements. In these groups, often made up of single-parent families, parent power is usually shared. To date there is not enough research available to know what the adaptations are likely to be.

Regardless of the kinds of power used in a family and the number of parents or parent surrogates, children experience injunctions—commands, directives, orders—about themselves and their value and about what to expect from the rest of the world.

They experience both the *words* of the injunctions and the *feelings* behind the words. They also experience the power that is used to enforce them. "You can do it" can be said with an encouraging voice or in a threatening manner. Children adapt to their parents' feelings, not only in hearing the verbal messages but in using their intuition to interpret the more important message behind the words. It is this energy of the parent power that is so spellbinding.

Notes from a Workshop

Bert came into a self-reparenting workshop in desperation. Bert grew up with irrational parents and described how he adapted to a situation that had no rules:

"I've always been afraid of going crazy. My mother was. About every year or so she would be put in the hospital as a raving maniac. My father didn't pay any attention to me at all unless he got drunk and acted crazy in his way.

"I could always come and go as I wanted. There were no rules. I used to get into all kinds of trouble. At school I'd get the teachers mad at me, and then the cops would come around and everything was chaos. Then I got into drugs and got crazier—and got into all kinds of fights about nothing.

"Man, I really need to change myself and get myself together. Even my girl-friend told me I had crazy, wild eyes. I really think I need some limits set on me so I don't turn out like my parents did. But if somebody else, like my probation officer, sets the limits, I'll probably flip again. I need my own lim-its. I need a good parent inside my head."

Jack, a controlled thirty-year-old who was also in the workshop, spoke from the opposite point of view:

"I need just the opposite kind of parent. All my life I've been 'Daddy's good little boy.' I've always done what 'Little Jackie' was supposed to do.

"I've complied, and complied, and complied. Now I'm going to change. I'm going to tell my dad to lay off, that I'm not 'Little Jackie' any more. I'm go-ing to plan it carefully and tell him when we're alone, and I'm really going to do it. I've had more than enough of his controlling ways. I'm going to flat out rebel. . . ."

Sonja, also in the workshop, interrupted: "How would you dare do that? I wouldn't. My parents would feel terrible if I talked back to them. My mom would cry, and my dad would withdraw and be silent for days, and then I'd start to feel guilty. Then Mom would ring me up and complain for hours about Dad, and then I'd go see them and try my best to make them happy and, as usual, I wouldn't succeed. The only way I'll ever escape to freedom is to move a long way away from my parents, but I keep putting it off and procrastinating as usual."

Obedience to Authority

Harmonious relationships in families require each person to obey certain rules, laws, and customs. However, when children are taught to obey blindly, without thinking, it interferes with their capacity to make intelli-gent judgments in later life. It is widely accepted, almost universally accepted, that it is not fair to cause another person to suffer who is not harmful or threatening to others. Yet a recent, devastating study shows that many people will harm others when an authority tells them to do so.

In a scientifically controlled laboratory setting where the conditions could be carefully observed, a psychological experiment was designed by Stanley Milgram to study obedience and disobedience to authority. The aim of the experiment was to find when and how people would defy authority in the face of a clear moral imperative.

The process of the experiment was to find out under what conditions —*when there is no threat of any sort*—a person would obey or disobey if instructed to hurt another person with a series of electrical shocks of increasing severity. The person being shocked was an actor who was well able to simulate suffering. The "authority" was the experimenter who would order the shock to be increased. To get out of the situation, the obedient shocker would have to make a clean break against authority. The choices made were devastating. Usually it was to obey the authority and hurt others.

Readers of that study might say, "Oh no, not me." That kind of hurtful action would not fit their self-image. They would, according to Milgram, be convinced that when confronted with a choice between hurting others and complying with authority, normal people reject authority. Some of the critics of the study are doubly convinced that Americans in particular do not act inhumanely against their fellows on the orders of authority. The fact is, they do and did. Many people commit terrible crimes, against themselves and against others, in the name of obedience.

This raises some difficult problems in parenting because in any form of communal living, some power, some form of authority, is used. Obedience is the most common response and explains why people will obey political leaders whether or not their actions are ethical. Learning to obey parental figures without question starts in childhood. It is a conditioning process that often leaves people feeling helpless in later life unless someone is telling them what to do.

Parents prefer obedient to disobedient children, yet obedience can serve an evil cause; witness the history of systematic destruction of people through wars, socioeconomic exploitation, and cult mass suicides. Yet, disobedience or rebellion is often punished in childhood. And although children may *feel* triumphant when they rebel, at the same time they may be fearful of the consequences. Thus the decision of whether to obey or rebel or procrastinate is a major childhood crisis.

Learning to Obey

As you relax and let your memory drift back in time, see yourself in a situation where you felt it was necessary to obey some authority figure. Was it a healthy or unhealthy obedience?

Obedience to Authority Takes Many Forms

National Archives

Pearson

"Some day when we grow up."   "I hope I do it right."

"What are the choices?"

Pearson

What did you do? What did you expect would happen by obeying? Do you still try to act in similar ways?

Styles of Obedience

Many adaptations interfere with the creation of a new self. Among these are five typical behavior patterns of complying to authorities that people tend to select in childhood. They are "drivers" that parents give their children to encourage obedience. They often become styles, for life. According to psychologist Tabie Kahler, the drivers, given verbally or nonverbally, are: Try hard, Be perfect, Hurry up, Please me, and Be strong.

"Try hard" says the parent to the young child sitting on the toilet or getting dressed or taking medicine or eating meals. "I'm trying," says the child tearfully or angrily. "Don't you see how hard I'm trying, but I can't do it." "Try harder," says the parent. "I can't, I can't. It's too hard," responds the child.

Later in life, "trying hard" may be a driving force in that person's life. Some people who try hard actually achieve very difficult goals. Others just go on trying and seldom achieve their purposes. They often feel incompetent, even dumb and stupid.

"Be perfect" or "Do it over until you get it right," says the parent to the young child who makes normal mistakes. "I'm trying," says the child, "but I can't get it good enough. I'll never be good enough." And so the sense of inferiority begins.

Later in life, persons with "be perfect" drivers may attempt only things they can do perfectly and also, from the Parent ego state, expect perfection from others. In some cases, people who continually try to be perfect lose both their will and their hope that anything could ever change.

"Hurry up," "Hurry up," "Hurry up," says the impatient parent to a child who is not interested in hurrying. "I'm coming as fast as I can," a child may retort. "I *am* hurrying. Don't you see?"

Later in life, persons with "hurry up" drivers continually rush from one thing to another. In their hurry, they may have accidents, create messes, make mistakes, and overlook important issues.

"Please me," "Make me happy," says the "poor me" parent who is emotionally inadequate and puts the responsibility on children to create happiness by being good, quiet, polite, and pleasing.

Later in life, persons with the drive to please others continually defer, give in, and avoid conflict. They often experience strong guilt feelings if they do not measure up to what they imagine other people want.

"Be strong" comes from the parent who is against the expression of feelings or against the expression of certain feelings. Many parents say things such as, "Big boys don't cry," and their children may adapt by withholding tears and acting tough and strong. Other parents say things such as, "Nice girls don't get angry," and their children may adapt by withholding their anger and crying instead.

Later in life, persons with "be strong" drivers may not take care of themselves physically or may deny their emotions. In relationships, they may act strong and attract weak people whom, in time, they criticize for being as they are. Or they may act so strong that it becomes a challenge to others who may try to beat them down. In either case, it is not unusual for a be-strong person to be a loner, with few friends.

Each of these addictions to driver behavior interferes with freely using intuition and creativity to find new paths to freedom and joy.

Rebellion against Authority

Rebellion against authority often shows itself in early childhood. Children learn defiance at an early age. "No" or "I won't" is often first heard from two-year-olds and is one of the earliest signs of the drive for personal identity.

"I won't" are words commonly used to assert one's identity, to say "No" to an unreasonable request, to stand up for important values in the face of possible rejection or repression.

"I won't" and "No" are favorite expressions of two- and three-year-olds who are becoming aware of their own needs and desires. These needs and desires may be just the opposite of those of their parents who, of course, "know best." "I want you to pick up your toys," one parent might shout. "I won't, I won't!" a child may shout back. "Don't you dare talk to me like that!" may be the next parental command. The child's rebellion and tears may then escalate to a temper tantrum. The parent becomes angrier and the reward may be a threat, "I'll give you something to cry about," and then a spanking.

And thus it goes that people learn to comply to force and power or to *appear* to comply to force and power, when actually they may be saying to themselves, "I won't. And when I get a chance, I'll show them."

Defiance is an attitude, sometimes expressed in bold or insolent ways, sometimes in soft and procrastinating ways. Regardless of the mask it wears, defiance is an attempt to be free from authoritarian demands. Parents are often upset by defiance. Some call it "stubbornness" and try to placate or punish the stubborn one into obedience. Others may call it "guts" and compliment a child who takes the "try and make me" bravado stance. Still other parents feel powerless, turn away from the situation, and throw up their hands in dismay. Feeling helpless and without parent power, they lose their ability to be adequate models and to influence their children effectively.

The person who experiences dissatisfaction with the human state of affairs and with her or his own place in the universe may perform simple acts of defiance, like a child who refuses to cooperate by throwing a temper tantrum or withdrawing. Dissatisfaction may also lead to an anarchistic state of mind, which can hold danger for the individual, as well as for those whose authority is opposed or resented. In a healthier way, dissatisfaction can lead to deciding to change and to discovering the personal power to do so. Change inevitably involves choosing for the future while owning up to the past.

An increasing number of families have lives filled with confusion and chaos. A family with chaos and lawlessness encourages criminal behavior and going crazy. The parents may be so irrational that the children reject them and their power. Later in life they may reject all other forms of authority, refusing to discriminate between what is rational and what is irrational. Such people live under two power myths: that all power and authority is bad, and that when some people have authority, it always leads to a decrease in other's freedom.

Rebellion has elements of defiance yet it is not anarchy. It is an open, organized resistance to authority based on a rational understanding of the person(s) or situation that is being rebelled against. There is no consensus as to what forms of behavior constitute healthy or unhealthy forms of rebellion, but it can be readily seen that is human life would not grow and change were it not for a spirit of rebellion that is inherent to human experience. People such as Gandhi emerge from a sense of rebellion; so do countries such as the United States. Rebellion stems from dissatisfaction with the status quo.

Choosing to Rebel

Think over your childhood—the times you had daydreams about rebelling and the times you actually rebelled.

What preceded your rebelling?

What did you hope to gain by rebelling?

Do you still rebel in similar ways?

Procrastination Responses

Some people do not make up their minds whether to rebel or comply, so they develop a life-style of procrastination.

"Next week I'll turn it in, teacher . . . "

"I'll do it after dinner, father . . . "

"Just a few more minutes, mother . . . "

These are often common delaying tactics by a child who wants to say "No!" and doesn't dare. It is a way of using personal power to block the power of others. It delays change indefinitely.

When children procrastinate they are trying to satisfy the inner war between "No, I won't" and "Yes, I will." Procrastination is a compromise. "Just a minute" or "I'll do it later" seems to them like a safer way to ignore authorities than saying "No."

If their parents insist on obedience, they may become angry. *"I didn't ask to be born"* is a typical angry response of children who experience pain, either physical or psychological, for much of their childhood. They feel helpless and without strength. As unhappy children they may lash out with "I wish I was dead" or "Don't blame me. I didn't ask to be here."

Such children may run away, or want to run away. Or they may act in ways so that their parents wish they would leave. Such a parent might complain, "That kid's going to be the death of me yet. I wish he would get out." Although many children occasionally use statements such as "I didn't ask to be born" to manipulate their parents into feeling guilty, when they do this frequently it is a symptom that they feel unwanted and unloved and may be moving from compliance and procrastination to defiance and rebellion.

Grown-ups who procrastinate and get angry at themselves or others also feel unwanted and unloved. "Nobody appreciates me" is the way it may be expressed verbally. At a nonverbal level they may say to themselves, "It's not my fault. I didn't ask to be born." They may then fantasize dramas where everyone would be sorry if they died.

"Everything I do is wrong" or *"I never do anything right"* are frequently heard from people who procrastinate while feeling depressed. As children they may have tried to do everything perfectly, discovered it was impossible, yet didn't change their modus operandi. So they go on trying to be "nice" or "good" or "the best" or "perfect." As adults they may sink into depression, become highly competitive to avoid their internal depression, or demand so much perfection from themselves that they put off getting started. After all, they expect to fail.

"I wouldn't dare" or *"Oh, I couldn't say that"* are phrases some people use when they don't speak up on their own behalf. They may assume others are too fragile and too easily hurt to hear anything that remotely seems like the truth. Or they imagine only a critical response to their honesty, so they too procrastinate, day after day, and avoid solving problems.

"Who cares? Why bother?" are other typical delaying phrases. Like someone treading water, these people never seem to get ahead. Figuratively speaking, although their legs and feet move up and down and they appear to be active, they are only staying in place, acting passive, waiting for further commands which they intend to reject just as they have rejected other suggestions.

Procrastination is often a sign of a spellbound child who has not learned how to make decisions and uses helplessness and confused feelings to

Procrastination is Disguised Rebellion

Hebble

James

"Nuts to you!"

"No one's going to tell me
what to do."

"Do I have to?"

"I am not procrastinating."

Hebble

Hebble

dramatize the lack of freedom. When procrastination becomes a life-style, it also becomes a major problem.

Notes from a Workshop

Sam, a forty-year-old business executive, was competent on the job and incompetent in relating to his wife.

"It seems like we had a constant power struggle going on between us. I thought I was supposed to be boss of the house but she refused to let me. She said, 'Go be boss on the job. Here we need to be equal.' I just wouldn't change. She pleaded, begged, implored—even got bossy herself. Then she threatened to leave if I didn't treat her as a grown-up woman instead of a child."

"Well, I planned to do it. I said I would go to counseling and stop being so bossy. I've been *saying* that for three years and *doing* nothing about it. Now she's left. She said she's tired of waiting, tired of my procrastinating."

Procrastination as a Life-Style

If you see yourself as very compliant, you may also be apt at procrastination when in fact you really want to rebel.

Consider how and when you procrastinated in childhood. Was it a general pattern or related to specific issues or people?

Do you have similar patterns in your current life? What might your good, new inner parent advise?

Addictions to Life-Styles

The word *addiction* is usually associated with narcotics, and when a person is said to be addicted, it commonly refers to one who is "hooked" on drugs. Being hooked means being so attached to something that it is almost impossible to get away—like a fish caught by the appeal of the bait and a strong hook. Many people think of themselves as powerful or as powerless. Few people think of themselves as addicted. They do not abuse themselves by misusing drugs so they tend to think of themselves as free. Yet the word *addict* does not just mean a person on drugs. It refers to all people who habitually or compulsively devote themselves to something.

People have many addictions. They are addicted to their values and ideas, to their jobs, their families, their life-styles, certain foods, places, people, objects, and so forth. They may feel as if they "can't stand it" or "could hardly live" without having what they are addicted to. The addiction may be to a continuous type of behavior—obedience, rebellion, or procrastination.

More than the feelings of wishing and wanting, which most people can tolerate, feelings of being addicted lead to the decision to do "almost anything" because the habit and craving is so intense. Deciding to "do almost anything" to satisfy the craving often requires creativity. Some children are very "creative" in getting what they want. They become artists of manipulation. Instead of voicing their needs directly, they may hint with a pouting lower lip or a tear or two.

If they discover that their hinting does not work, they may be creative in more obvious ways, like having a temper tantrum, getting a stomachache, bursting out into sobs. Eventually they collect enough information about what to do to get what they want. Knowingly or unknowingly they make decisions to become skilled at this particular "act" they have chosen. This often becomes part of their personality and life-style, which, as they grow up, they become addicted to. For example, being addicted to membership in the Dumb and Ugly Club leads to patterns that perpetuate the dumb and ugly self-image. Addictions are observable in compulsive behavior or compulsive thinking. It is as though people are listening to their internal drivers which compel them to go in certain habit patterns that interfere with their freedom to update the old self and develop a new self.

Avoiding Freedom

To avoid changing, many people hold fast to their belief that they are unable to take charge of their own lives or, even if they are able, they refuse to do so. "I can't" or "I don't know how" are favorite excuses.

"I can't" is a common response some people make when they are confronted with problems. "I can't" may be said with a whine as children sometimes use

when they have demands made upon them that they don't like or that are beyond their capacities. "I can't" may or may not be true.

In many parts of the world people really "can't." They are chattel, bought and sold like oxen or other beasts of burden, unable to have control over their own lives. They are exploited sexually, psychologically, or economically. In other parts of the world people claim they can't to avoid the challenges of breaking free.

"I don't know how" are words that are often used to disguise the "I can't" lament. Frequently they are a pretext to avoid learning something new.

> "I can't fix the car because I don't know how."
>> "I can't get a job because I don't know how."
>>> "I can't have fun because I don't know how."

Many people discover in early childhood that acting helpless often brings helpful people to their rescue. Then they do not have to take charge of their own lives. They do not have to affirm their potential *courage to be*, nor do they have to call on their *courage to do* and risk potential failure or potential success.

These people attach themselves to others who appear to be strong, who will help them and take care of them and make their decisions for them. Thus they can remain safely dependent. So they imagine! In time, dependency leads to symbiosis, which leads to resentments. Both the "helpless" one and "helpful" one may feel trapped in the relationship and resentful of it.

In addition to being a disguise for "I can't," the "I don't know how" may also be a mask for "I won't."

> "I don't know how to fix the faucet (so I won't try)."
>> "I don't know how to get a job (so I won't try)."
>>> "I don't know how to have fun (so I won't try)."

Sometimes this is healthy if it means, "I won't let you direct my life. I'll do it myself," or "I won't put so much energy into trying to be perfect and pleasing everyone. I'll be easier on myself."

Sometimes the "I won't" is merely the rebellious opposite of "I can't." In such cases a person's energy is not directed toward a positive getting on with life. Instead it's directed in a negative fashion—against others.

Sometimes "I don't know how" is part fact, part fiction. For example, persons who want to lose weight may know that they need to eat less (fact). However, they may claim that in spite of all the information available, they do not know what they need to eat less of (fiction).

"*I don't know how, yet*" is a more creative position. The "yet" implies the possibility of new goals and the possibility of finding out how to reach those goals. Said another way it would be, "I know that I don't know, and I know I can find out." This kind of statement affirms both being and doing and the courage to change that is required for breaking free. Breaking free often requires moral decisions that are not easy to make.

The Morality of Obedience and Rebellion

In the widespread sensate culture of today, many people avoid thinking or talking about ethical problems and moral issues, yet people live by them whether they know it or not.

The words "morals" and "ethics" are often used interchangeably. Both are concerned with values. Both are concerned with judgments of what is right or wrong, good or bad, in character and behavior.

Ethics are *general principles* believed to be true by some part of society regarding what is right and what is wrong. Morals, however, are *personal, individual opinions* on what is right and wrong, rather than the opinions of a group. When a person goes against an accepted group ethic, it is often because of a personal moral decision.

Naturally, group opinions affect individuals and visa versa. Yet moral decisions do not easily change although what is defined as ethical may be redefined whenever the values of a group change. For example, physicians and teachers are expected to be ethical in specific ways. Until recently, physicians were not supposed to advertise; teachers were not supposed to use corporal punishment. These were parts of the ethical codes of their professions. Now, although many will not do so, physicians are allowed to advertise and teachers are, in some cases, allowed to use corporal punishment. The new standards reflect changed values.

Obedience to a group ethic may be viewed by those inside the group as moral and by those outside as immoral. For example, in the recent clash with Iran the two sides could not understand the other side's ethical position. Each labeled the other "immoral." So too the ethics of a nation may favor military power. Yet a conscientious objector may refuse to fight. As a third example, a gang of delinquents may attack someone who is weak and a passerby may try to rescue the attacked one. The attempt to rescue is based on a moral decision of what is right or wrong, good or bad. The delinquents, who may have their own code of behavior for their gang, are likely to be considered immoral by others.

Teachers, parents, and other authority figures often try to inculcate morals by lecturing at people and by using moralistic, simplistic platitudes and the repetitive use of slogans. However well meaning they are, the platitudes and slogans are more likely to serve as a *control* over children's behavior than as a tool for teaching them how to think about problems that are involved with moral issues.

Learning how to think is not the same as being educated. Some educated people merely parrot what they have learned in school, whereas a person who thinks may be quite critical of the curriculum and instructors and may be able to objectively point out errors in information and judgment and make decisions that reflect a high morality.

Morals are best learned by observing good models as well as by learning how to think abstractly. Unfortunately the moral remarks people make often do not match their behavior. This is obvious even to children who are admonished, "Don't cheat," yet observe their parents cheating in many ways. Children with this experience may conclude it's permissible to cheat but not permissible to get caught. If they don't rethink this incongruity as they grow up, they will stay at one of the lower levels of moral development, often procrastinating between obedience and rebellion. Recent interest in value clarification in schools is an effort to help children recognize their values and the moral decisions they make regarding them.

Interesting research by Lawrence Kohlberg indicates that moral development in people possibly occurs in a sequence of six developmental steps, even as physical, psychological, and intellectual growth occurs in steps.

Obedience out of fear of punishment is the first stage of moral development. The infant, wanting to avoid physical pain or discomfort, learns early in life that it is wise to adapt to parental demands. Obeying authority figures is felt to be right, not because the authorities are right but because they have the power to punish. Therefore, "staying out of trouble" to avoid punishment is what is important.

Some people, mistreated in childhood, have great difficulty moving beyond this stage of moral development. They live a lifetime of fear and obey, often without thinking, and are afraid that a spouse, peer, an organized crime group, or a government might punish them physically if they do not conform.

Satisfying one's own needs from a materialistic position is the second stage of moral development. Young children as budding opportunists enter this when they discover they have power over their own bodies and therefore over part of their lives. At this stage, what they can do and not get punished for, such as taking a forbidden cookie or toy, becomes the measure of what is considered right. "It must be right," reasons the young child, "if my needs are satisfied."

Also at this stage is concern for reward; that if rules are obeyed, there should be some kind of benefit in return. "You scratch my back and I'll scratch yours" (but I want more scratching than I'm willing to give you), is the norm for this stage. "Me and my needs, always first" is the orientation.

As children grow up they may continue at this level or, from time to time, revert to it, stealing candy bars from stores or money from mom's purse, testing the system. In grown-ups this is often observed in the world of business. Companies may decide it's advantageous to dump pollutants in a river, if they can get away with it. Individuals may steal time or money from the company or from the family because of the narcissistic attitude of "What *I* want, legal or illegal, is what I'm going to try to get, if I can get away with it."

These first two stages are typical of young children because they do not understand the whys and wherefores of rules. The next two stages reflect conventional morality. The possible recognition of this begins in early school years.

Pleasing others to get approval is common at this time. Children who develop to this stage are often called "nice." They are easy to manage because they want to be considered "good." They act so that they will be seen in that light, and what they consider to be moral is what parents and teachers would approve of.

In grown-ups, this nonquestioning behavior of pleasing others is sometimes noticeable in people who are not assertive when they need to be. They believe that obedience to some cultural norm to earn approval from others is more important than breaking free. This stage of moral development is also noticeable when people work on jobs they don't like or don't respect but stick to because they receive compliments, money, or title that reflects approval by the boss. So too in marriages and friendships, some people stay in them when they don't want to. They continually try to please others and often may not succeed. Eventually this may lead to anger.

Obeying established law and order comes next. Learning the rules and following rules in games and other activities is the focus of this development, which is common beginning at age nine. Pledging loyalty out of a sense of duty is a common expression of this stage. Behavior is considered right if it complies with the law and order of the cultural or subcultural group.

In grown-ups, this stage of moral developent shows in people who "continually" do what a country, company, union, family, or religious organization tells them what is right and what they "should" do. They are obedient and compliant and respect authority at this level of moral development and pay their bills and so forth from a *sense of duty*, not because of the fear of punishment. "I *should* go home on time. That's what's expected; it's my duty" says the nine-year-old or perhaps the thirty-nine-year-old who believes the status quo is right.

Respecting constitutionally granted rights because of a system of laws while believing laws can be rationally changed instead of rigidly maintained, is the next stage of moral development. It is possible, though not probable or common for this to begin between ages sixteen and twenty, because at this age people are able to think abstractly about principles and human rights. Intense involvement, especially of young people in political issues, stems from the belief that laws can and should be changed so they "protest" current law by picketing. Of course some who are politically active are merely against authority and, given the chance, would prefer anarchy. The key to this stage is *rational* change of unjust laws and mutual agreements by social contracts.

Concern for universal ethical principles is the highest stage of moral development. It is not based on a system of laws but on the need for truth, justice, and beauty, and the values and dignity of human life. Schwitzer is an example of someone who reached this stage. Not many people do. This orientation requires the capacity to develop principles and to think theoretically and analytically. It also requires the willingness to live consistently on

There are Stages in Moral Development

James

"I hope they like the way I am."

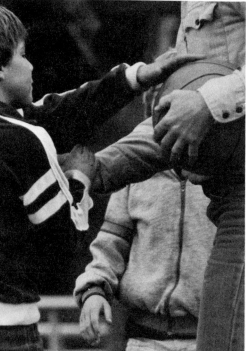

Hebble

James

"I pledge allegiance . ."

"Let's play fair."

"Decisions can be made by vote."

National Archives

the basis of self-chosen principles even in a less than perfect society and, when making moral decisions, to weigh all factors and decide on the basis of the situation, not necessarily on the basis of law, to fight against unfairness, even to die for principles of truth and justice.

One of the thought-provoking discoveries of Kohlberg's studies was that most people are stuck en route because they have not conquered the tasks required to think clearly. The implications are obvious. It is more important for children to learn *how* to think than to obediently learn *what* to think by agreeing with parents' slogans. Unless people are able to think abstractly, such as considering the value of *life* versus the value of possessions, they do not achieve full moral development. Instead they make moral decisions on the basis of "the path of least resistance" and do not use their vitality for breaking free.

One of the things some people discover about themselves when doing self-reparenting is that they stopped growing at one level of moral development connected with certain issues and continued to grow in relation to other issues. For example, some people may drive cars in ways that are definitely life-threatening to themselves and others (stuck at the second level of the opportunist, hoping not to be caught), and are very nice to others in their immediate circle of family, friends, and colleagues (third stage). This inconsistency shows some lack of caring and thinking about what it would mean to be whole, living a new life of authenticity.

In the long and painful history of liberation there are those leaders— whether known or not—who act with the courage of their convictions and live by universal principles that enhance the lives of all. The moral decisions of people who achieve this stage are not rigid; they are flexible. Their values often change in light of changing situations. They use their vitality in positive ways to fight for a better world. They do not give in passively when national or world situations seem disastrous.

People whose moral development has stopped in some areas need to find new models or design new parent messages for breaking free. They need to reevaluate their responses to the authority of others and to the authority of themselves.

Breakthrough IV—Comparing Life-Styles

This chapter has focused on the basic ways children adapt to authorities and to their demands for obedience. The purpose of this breakthrough is to allow you to own up to your parents and their life-styles so you can see the similarities and differences you have created for yourself. Fill in the following sentences:

My Parents' Life-Style: If I were to describe the life-style our family lived when I was a child, I would say it was _____ and _____ and _____ because _____ _____.

This life-style was conducive to freedom in the following ways: _____ _____.

It was not conducive to freedom in the following ways: _____ _____.

My Life-Style: My life-style five years ago was similar to that of my parents in the following ways: _____.

It was different from that of my parents in the following ways: _____.

When I now evaluate the life-style I lived five years ago, I think _____ _____ and feel _____.

My *present* life-style could be compared with _____ _____.

It is like the life-style my parents once lived in the following ways: _____ _____.

It is unlike their life-style in the following ways: _____ _____.

Some of the ways it pleases me are _____ _____.

What I would like to change is _____ _____.

The potential cost of changing is _____.

In view of this potential cost, I [will] [will not] change my life-style.

To do this, I would need to be a good parent to myself by _____ _____.

Values and Life-styles Sometimes Change

National Archives

"I wish we had another boy."

"Wow, I like my job!"

"One is just perfect for me."

Hebble

Jefferey

Evaluating Moral Decisions: Discover when and how you make moral decisions on the basis of compliance, obedience, or procrastination by considering the following questions:

In what situations do I make moral decisions because of fear of punishment?

In what situations do I make decisions on an opportunistic basis of what comes along or what I can get away with?

In what situations do I decide what to do on the basis of pleasing others?

In what situations do I decide on the basis of "that's the law" or "of course that's the order of things"?

Am I concerned over constitutional rights and in working to change unjust laws? If so, in what ways?

Am I, or am I planning to be, actively concerned with universal human rights while accepting the possibility that other peooples' definition of human rights may be more "right" than mine?

Excuses for Not Changing: Let your memory drift back to situations in childhood at home or school when you felt unable to meet certain demands or challenges given by authorities.

Relive your feelings. Hear your words. How did you respond in words and actions?

Now consider current situations and your patterns of response. How are your excuses similar and different from those in your childhood?

What new inner parent messages do you need for your new life?

 Now in your journal summarize your awareness of freedom in your life-style.

The Stress of Unmet Needs

5

There is no freedom for the weak.
Meredeth

Many people do not know how to be good parents to themselves because they are not aware of what they really want or need. Some fail in reparenting because they refuse to admit the importance of their needs. Still others experience inner turmoil when what they want ("I *want* to go out and have fun tonight") and what they need ("but I'm so tired, I *need* to go to bed") are not in harmony. They may also feel stress when their desires are in conflict with what other people want or need. They often feel weak instead of strong. Consequently the stress may build up to dangerous levels. To reduce stress it is necessary to determine the causes, the responses, and the possible solutions.

In this step of self-reparenting, you will become more aware of your childhood needs and wants. You will discover the similarities and the differences between the way you felt them in childhood and the way you feel them now. You will also become more aware of how stress develops when needs and wants are not met.

Recognizing your stress and stress responses will show you what your new parent needs to be like so that you can relax and still get what will enhance your life.

You will also learn how to use your Adult ego state as a substitute parent and enter into a dialogue with your inner Child. This dialogue technique will be permanently useful as you continue breaking free. The new parent you are developing for yourself will learn how to recognize and deal with stress.

Needs and Wants Differ

Needs are what is necessary either for existence itself or for being successful at living. They are what persons know intuitively or by experience that they *must* have just to stay alive. People cannot indefinitely starve, and they know it. Nor can they go indefinitely without sleep. Bodily needs *must* be met, yet many people's needs are met only at a survival level.

"Nobody loves me" is a typical nonfree response of children whose needs for affection are not met. They may have some awareness of what they need, yet not know how to get it. When grown up, they may have a vague feeling that something is missing inside and always has been missing, yet not know what that something is. Some of these people go through life seeking out others to parent them in one way or another to compensate for their inability to parent themselves. They act helpless, angry, confused, or inadequate and elicit parental nurturing or criticism from others.

Still others, who may also feel unlovable, may decide to resist an inner urge to seek parent figures. They don't believe others could have a sense of parental caring for them. Therefore they often resent anyone whom they interpret as taking that role. They are not free to taste the riches of relationships. Sometimes these people are willing to nurture others but are not willing to accept nurturing for themselves. Being in control is such a high priority for them, they only trust themselves.

When these two kinds of people—those who search anxiously for parenting and those who resist parenting from others—reparent themselves, they can love themselves. When they love and take care of themselves they accept the reality that they are lovable and "of course" others will care for them. They discover the need for freedom.

Although the word *wants* is sometimes used interchangeably with *needs*, I am using it here to refer to what a person wishes for or desires. Meeting these desires is not necessary for existence but may be necessary for what is called "the quality of life."

People often confuse what they want with what they need. "I really want a new dress" may become such a consuming desire that a person acts as though life depended on getting this particular desire met.

Notes from a Workshop

"What I want," said Joe, after a long day at work, "is just to sit quiet and be left alone. I don't want to deal with family problems when I first get home. My wife says that's what I *need* to do. Well, that's her need; it's not mine. I *need* to sit quietly and just relax as my body is too tense. And I also *want* to just sit."

"Well, I *want* to sit, too!" exploded Judith, his wife. "But how can I when the kids are fighting and the dog is barking and the plumbing gets plugged up? I also *need* to feel as if you're on my side and willing to help me, not just into your own thing. Don't you see? I feel as if I need your involvement so much and I can't stand it if I don't get it. It isn't a 'want'; it's a need."

"Well, I've got needs, too," said Joe with a tone of resignation. "Apparently my needs don't matter."

"Oh, Joe, that's not fair!" Judith retorted, "you always come first with me and you know it."

And so it goes, the battle of needs versus wants, or of one person's needs being more important than the other person's. As the battle rages, stress grows and judgments about whose needs or desires are most important begin to surface.

Enslaved by Unmet Needs

Unmet basic or growth needs often act as chains that interfere with a feeling of freedom. In a sense all people are slaves, at least to their own bodies. They may try to "own" and control them. Eventually the body rules; the cells die. For rich or poor, educated or not, free or enslaved, death comes. Some look forward to this as a liberation; others dread the prospect as the final "solitary confinement."

Children who have grown up in war-torn countries may learn restriction of bodily movement as a way of life. *The Diary of Anne Frank*, written by a

Survival and Stress are Closely Linked

"Any way out when all is gone?"

"Any way out
of the coal mines?"

"Any way out
from a concentration camp?"

young adolescent who lived for years in a garret hiding from Nazi troopers, testifies to the fear and courage of many. Those who have fled from war-torn or dictatorship-controlled countries testify to another kind of courage in the face of fear. And those who spend years trying to survive in concentration camps often reflect a quality of glory because of their courage.

For many who are not in chains or behind bars, the struggle to exist physically is almost as exhausting and terrifying. Plagues, starvation, and painful death are worldwide sores that fester in spite of high technological skills.

Less dramatic, though no less real, is life-debilitating poverty, the poverty that destroys muscle tissue and organ functioning and the capacity to think and change and grow. I remember well the two times in my life when I had little to eat, was emaciated, and in fear of starvation. My fear was that "there may be no way out of this terror."

People whose bodies are disintegrating with age or disease or whose bodies do not function well because of accident often experience the same kind of terror and despair that I knew.

Many people reading this book have had different experiences. They have not been slaves, or prisoners, or lived in ghettos, or spent much time in hospitals. Instead they have felt enslaved to other kinds of needs or desires that were just as intense. Each person's burden is one's own, and it often seems worse to the person who has it than the burdens of other people.

Your Childhood Needs and Wants

Let your memory drift back again to your childhood awareness of what you experienced as needs and what you experienced as wants and desires. Make a list of these.

Reflect on how they affected your life as you were growing up and how they may affect your life now.

Were they similar to the needs and wants of your parents? Were your parents able to get their own needs and wants met? If not, why not?

Were they "stuck" because of their internal personality problems or because of external situations over which they may not have had much control?

If they did get their needs and wants met, how did they do it? What were their techniques or strategies?

What implication does this have for you as you develop a new, good internal parent?

A System for Identifying Needs and Wants

If you were to list your current needs and wants, you would probably include some things that would make your physical existence more satisfying and some that would enhance your personal or professional life.

One very well-known system for understanding needs and wants was developed by psychologist Abraham Maslow who said people had five needs: physiological, safety, belonging, esteem, and self-actualizing. These can be diagramed on the basis of a triangle with the bottom physiological level of need as the foundation for subsequent development.

Physiological and safety needs are basic to existence. The other three are basic to growth and are what I call wants or desires rather than needs.

People can live without them if necessary, although the quality of their lives will suffer.

The following is based on the order of Maslow's needs because I think it is a useful system, yet it is also an expansion of his ideas. The expansion shows symptoms that reflect unmet needs and wants and points to specific areas for reparenting with the goal of breaking free.

The *physiological need* is experienced immediately after being born when the first struggle is for breath. When breathing is difficult, the struggle to breathe is sometimes continued through life. It may show in later years in a pattern of deep sighing.

The next struggle is to eat. Infants usually eat an appropriate amount unless they are criticized for being greedy or taking too long or are implored or forced to eat more. Many people unnecessarily use their mouths in later life to make up for what was lacking when they were little. They may continually put food, drink, drugs, or cigarettes in their mouths. These people are sometimes referred to as having the unmet basic oral needs of an infant. At an interpersonal level they may also "try to suck other people in" or "drain others dry," as though sucking on a baby bottle. Because they did not get what they needed in infancy, they may unknowingly remain enslaved to their past.

Some Things are More Basic Than Others

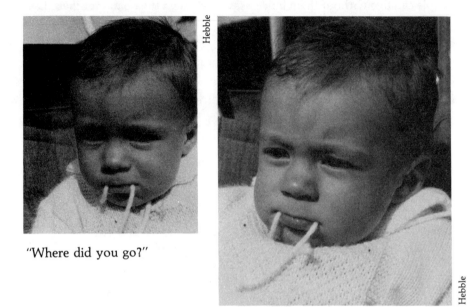

Hebble

"Where did you go?"

"Why did you stay so long?"

Hebble

"I'm glad you're back."

Hebble

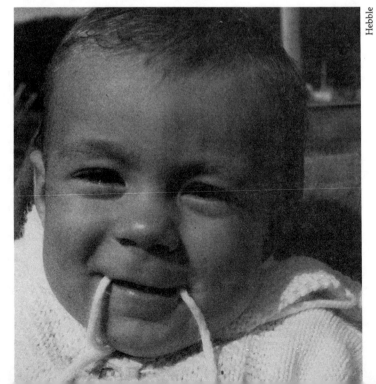

The *safety need* is another need that is difficult to live without. Without safety, the internal jailer is like a fearful monster that appears suddenly and grows to enormous heights. "I'm going to get you!" bellows the monster.

Signs that a person is enslaved to this include the continuing focus on accumulating wealth—gold, diamonds, money, and so forth—that can be used to "buy safety." Or preoccupation with locked windows and doors. Or attaching oneself in a symbiotic relationship to someone who is stronger. Or remaining in a "perfectly safe" though totally miserable job. Or being unwilling to go into new situations.

The sense of safety is closely related to physical needs. Hoarding food, for example, seems to some people a way to stave off the fear of starvation. Social agencies, assuming responsibilities for health care, stave off some of the fear of living and dying. The underlying dynamics for someone with a safety need is "I'm afraid," or "I don't trust people," or "I'll have to do it all myself."

The *desire to belong.*   Even if a person's basic physiological and safety needs are met, the grim specter of being alone and unloved is like solitary confinement. In fact, some people who have not had their needs for belonging met in childhood almost lock themselves off from others. "Don't get close to me" is the nonverbal message they may give to others. "Leave me alone" or "Don't bother me" or "I don't have time" is what they might say.

At the other extreme, some are desperate to belong. They "can't stand" being alone. They become "joiners" yet often feel as if they're on the fringe of the group. Clubs of all kinds are filled with people who want to belong. Some people seem to make it, some don't. Or as one woman put it, "I want two or more boyfriends; then if I lose one, I won't be alone."

The *desire for esteem.*   The continuous desire for praise and approval, the continuous struggle "up the organizational ladder," the search for a job with a higher title and more prestige, are symptoms. Persons who do this have little self-esteem. They are trying to bolster their egos, which actually feel shaky.

These people organize much of their energy to get public approval. The public might be a small group in the neighborhood or a large one at work. The message is the same: "Tell me I'm wonderful. I don't believe it but if you tell me often enough, who knows, I might—but I doubt it." Chained to the need for approval, these persons actually have low esteem.

The *desire for self-actualizing.*   People who are not involved in the process of self-actualizing often show this by their scattered interests or almost exclusive concern with themselves and their own ambitions. They care little for the rest of the world and abstract values such as justice, truth, and beauty. They may appear to be committed to something important but it's only for self-gratification.

They may dabble in art or politics, appearing to be interested in justice and beauty when they are not. They are amateurs, not professionals. They do not commit themselves to the discipline required for self-actualization. They need to start. Self-actualizing persons are self-starters. They do not wait to be encouraged or commanded. They "get places on their own steam."

You and Your Needs

Let memories of your childhood emerge from your past. Look at childhood photographs; picture your home and school. Recall your feelings of OK-ness and not-OK-ness. This will help you discover part of your inner Child that you may not be aware of.

Measuring Your Needs.   Ask yourself the following questions and check on each scale from 0 to 10 how your needs were met. Zero is low; ten is high:

Were your basic physiological needs (for water, food, clothing, air, etc.) met so that your body felt nourished?	0	10
Did you live in a situation and with people with whom you felt safe?	0	10
Did you usually feel loved and as if you belonged?	0	10
Did you esteem and approve of yourself and receive esteem and approval from others?	0	10
Did you feel independent and as if you were capable of self-actualization?	0	10

If you answered "yes" to each of the above questions, you have had a remarkable, unusual childhood. Most people are not that fortunate. They do not get all their needs met.

Everyone has Basic Needs

National Archives

"I need to be safe."

Stock, Boston, Inc.

"I need to succeed."

Pearson

"We need to belong!"

"We'll do the best we can do."

National Archives

Stress and the Stress Response

When people's physical or emotional needs are not met, they inevitably have a physical and emotional stress reaction. That which creates the situation is the stress or what is often called the stressor. The response is the *stress reaction.*

The best-known researcher on this subject is Hans Selye, author of many books, most of them on stress. He claims stress is the nonspecific response of the body to any specific demand, either positive or negative.

According to Selye, there are three steps of response: alarm, resistance, and exhaustion. First comes the sense of alarm when the body instinctively recognizes a stressor and responds biologically in ways that enable a person to fight against the demand or flee from it. Hormones are released in the bloodstream, changes occur in breathing patterns and heart rate, blood pressure often goes up. This is a basic response inherited from the days when physical flight was necessary to survive.

In the second stage, the body tries to adapt to the stress. If the stress stops, the body relaxes and repairs itself from damage caused by the stress. If the stress does not stop, the body continues its pattern of being "on alert" until exhaustion, the third step, sets in. With exhaustion a person often experiences headaches, profuse perspiration, rapid heartbeat, and so forth.

Stress can be a major problem if it becomes chronic. Then the body does not get a chance to achieve fully a state of homeostasis. Physical symptoms become more noticeable. Susceptibility to heart disease, ulcers, arthritis, and high blood pressure increases. The ability to fight back by having a strong immunological system may be lost.

Months, sometimes years, can pass before stress-related disease develops, yet there are many symptoms that stress is becoming intolerable. Some of these are nervousness, irritation, indecision, irrational anger, nausea during crisis, continuing fatigue, inability to sleep well, rigidity in facial muscles, jaw, or shoulders, grinding teeth, and nail biting. Indifference, passivity, and apathy are also signs that needs have not been met and that stress has been too high to cope with.

Notes from a Workshop

Denise, a mother of a cerebral palsied son, came to a self-reparenting workshop because of her growing indifferences to her child. She put it:

"I sort of just don't care any more. I kind of think that's wrong, but it's true. Some days I just don't care and on those days, I don't even feel guilty about *not* caring!

"My mother was the kind of person who took care of everybody else's needs—everybody except her own children. We were more like orphans. I made up my mind a long time ago not to be like that. I decided my kids would come first. However, it's not easy having a child like I have. Every time I take him out in his wheelchair, somebody stares. In the beginning I felt angry a lot. Then I felt so sad. Down to the bottom of my toes I felt sad. Now I'm beginning to feel indifferent. I don't like it. It's scary. I wish I had had a real mother who cared."

With that, Denise started whimpering, almost like a hurt puppy treated unfairly. In her decision to be a responsible parent, she had neglected her own needs and desires. Exhaustion was lowering her motivation to fight for her son. The stress had been too long, too constant.

Needs, Wants, and Stress

Consider your current situation. What are your physical and emotional signs of stress?

Are your ways of dealing with stress satisfying to you or not?

If not, what does that mean for you in your process of self-reparenting?

The Stress of Memories

Another thing that interferes with breaking free is the unwillingness or inability to give up past memories which often create continuing stress. Some terrors, such as concentration camps, may not be worked through. In such cases it may be best to put them aside and just let them be as part of the unpleasant past. It may not be possible.

In the storage house known as the brain are structures, only partly understood, that are involved in short-term, intermediary, and long-term memory processes. Memories may be readily accessible for easy replay or may be deeply buried. Sometimes the memories are simple to understand even if fragmentary. Sometimes they are not. The mind works in strange ways as, for example, when a person has a moment of déjà vu, which is being in a new situation with the strong feeling of having been there before.

Seemingly the mind acts somewhat like a camera and takes pictures of events, then stores them away. However the pictures are not only what is seen. The pictures include other sensory responses. For example, when looking at the "picture" of our family camping in the high Sierras, I can again feel the hardness of the granite rock that I sit on and the prickles of the pine needles where I lie down on my sleeping bag. I can smell the wood smoke and the bacon in the frying pan and hear the singing of old camp songs. Along with the sensory picture come emotions—feelings of anticipation, excitement, and joy. Also a replay of a judgment I made at the time that family camping is good.

In a very basic way, the memory process involves these three steps. First is the experience or the event. Next is the remembering and forgetting step, and third is the retention stage.

In self-reparenting the use of retention becomes very noticeable. People in this stage *recall* some of the past, *recognize* its familiarity, and *relearn* some forgotten techniques or learn new ones that can be used for a new life.

There are four basic views about why people may or may not remember much in spite of their experiences. The first view is that forgetting occurs because the learning has not been put to use. Many people comment on being unable to recall certain events or persons, places, numbers, and so forth with a complaint such as, "My mind went totally blank." This is a common experience for anxious exam takers when they have tried to memorize facts yet have not used the facts in some practical way nor applied the facts to other situations.

A different theory of forgetting is held by those who say that distortions of memory details occur because the original memory traces are transformed. A third view of remembering and forgetting is called the interference theory and is based on the belief that other events, occurring after the original events, interfere with the ability to recall the earlier one.

A commonly held psychoanalytic theory is based on the idea of "selective attention" and "selective inattention." This is said to be engineered at an unconscious or preconscious level. "I forgot our appointment" one person might say to another without the awareness of selecting to forget because of anticipated unpleasantness.

This kind of forgetting is commonly called repression—the ejection from consciousness of anxiety-related material. Although research shows that people tend to "forget" or repress unpleasant experiences more rapidly than neutral or pleasant events, it seems evident that choice is somehow involved. Perhaps the choice is related in some way to basic childhood responses in regard to authorities.

Some people who have become very compliant to others and then begin self-reparenting may not recall much of their childhood. Furthermore, they may only remember the positive aspects of their parent figures. Looking through rose-colored glasses, they may see themselves as continuously trying to please others and feel *self-righteous*.

Some people who begin self-reparenting, and who have chosen a rebelliousness as a behavior pattern, often give selective attention only to the negatives. Thus they can justify their *anger* and express their rage which they may have bottled up at an early age or not learned to control in reasonable ways.

Those who have chosen procrastination as a common way of delaying decisions and actions may remain unfocused and indecisive about what is important to remember and what is OK to forget. Feeling *guilty* for this use or nonuse of memory and behavior is often their most common feeling. It is not surprising that they may choose to "forget" the past.

Memories that Bless and Burn

Bring to mind something from your past that you often think about. Is it something that feels like a blessing or like a burn?

If the recurring memory hurts, what do you need your new parent to say to you so that you can heal?

The Stress of the Future

Future Shock and *The Third Wave*, popular books by Alvin Toffler, a writer about future stress, points to the many stresses people will inevitably face in the current race for technological superiority during "the death of industrialism and the rise of a new civilization". Whether people will make satisfying adaptations will greatly depend on whether their basic needs—for fresh air, food, water, clothing, and a place to sleep—will or will not be met, as well as whether they can change their old ways of thinking to fit the current facts. Futurology is a growing field inhabited by politicians, sociologists, scientists, and all the others who hypothesize what tomorrow will bring.

Many people think there is a real danger that their needs will not be met. They urge citizens to become aware of evacuation routes from big cities and of the catastrophic results that will occur in nuclear warfare. They fantasize total chaos and destruction.

Less fatal fantasies, yet also painful, are the economic fears of the future that point to things such as escalating inflation, fewer jobs, less available housing, and increased energy costs.

At a more personal level are the anxieties about one's body, friends, and families who are always in a state of change—breaking down, moving away, becoming alienated, or getting well, moving back, becoming intimate. Family styles, working styles, economics, and politics are all changing and change creates stress. Yet, a continual absorption on what *might* happen some day interferes with breaking free to live a new life now.

Because the stress reaction is a physical response to either positive or negative stressors, there are ways to use it for a positive outcome. Visualization is one of the most important techniques. It uses creative fantasies to visualize a positive outcome. For example, people who are overweight can learn to *see* themselves as thin and in control of what they eat. If the program is adhered to, the person loses weight. At a more dramatic level, the remission of cancer is sometimes possible with the assistance of relaxation visualizations—in brief, by seeing the cancer cells as being destroyed by stronger white cells and seeing themselves as well. Visualizations do change the body process.

They also change the psychological processes. People who see themselves with a future of continually helping others are likely to behave as if it was necessary. People who *see* themselves as obedient or rebellious or procrastinating in the future are likely to act that way in the now.

Living continually in anticipation of the future—whether good or bad—is to miss the excitement of now. Naturally the potential future needs to be recognized. After all, as simple a task as buying groceries often occurs because the need to eat at some future time is a realistic expectation. Yet living with energy continually focused on what will or might happen some day is a form of self-enslavement.

In the process of self-reparenting, a new parent within can say something like, "Yes, you do need to plan for the future—that cruise you want to take, the house you want to build, the friends you want to make—so, what are you going to do about it *now?* Do something now. Stop thinking about someday how 'your ship may come in' or 'your house may collapse some-day' or how 'someday you'll be all alone.' Many fears of the future will never occur so live life now."

Someday My Ship Will Come

The daydream of something like a personal ship coming in loaded with "jewels" is part of many people's lives (although currently they may prefer oil).

What are some of your positive hopes and negative fears? How much time and energy are you putting into them? Does your expenditure make sense? If not, what do you need to say to yourself?

The Stress of the Now

A popular belief held by many psychologists today is the importance of living in the now. Living in the now requires attention to experiencing body and emotions *now* instead of staying stuck in memories or expectations.

The value of being in the now is that a person's energy becomes focused. Fearful fantasies of what did or may have happened in the past or catastrophic fears or grandiose expectations of what might happen in the future lose much of their power to keep a person enslaved. However, living in the now is not easy. It requires decision and energy to monitor old Parent messages often directed to the past or the future such as:

"I almost died when you were born."

"We gave you everything when you were little."

"Be careful what you say when you go out in public."

"You can't trust tomorrow. It may not come."

It also requires becoming aware of and turning off the inner Child that rehearses what will be said and done in future situations or rehashes what was said and done in the past:

"I never do anything right."

"I said the wrong thing again."

"She'll never forgive me."

"When I see him I'm going to tell him . . ."

One of the most effective ways for living in the now was developed by Fritz Perls, a Gestalt therapist. He advocated staying in touch with one's senses. When doing this, it is almost impossible to review the past compulsively or rehearse for the future compulsively.

One of the easy Gestalt ways of maintaining bodily and sensory awareness is with the phrase, "Now I am aware . . . (of my breathing, my heartbeat, the odors in the room, the sound of the plane overhead, and so forth)." Runners seem to do this automatically. They experience themselves in the now. The now, of course, is always changing and the unfinished business of the past, as well as anticipations of the future, continuously enter the foreground of awareness. There it shapes up into a current problem, which, if solved, fades away.

Often meditation, autogenic training, or biofeedback training, which involves learning how to control one's brain waves, helps alleviate the stress of anxiety. So does using as simple a technique as the "Adult Leveling Position." This is sitting in a straight chair with feet flat on the floor, hands open on each leg, chin parallel to the floor, and head straight, not tipped either sideways or up and down. Whatever techniques are used, the new inner parent needs to remind the person, "Live in the now. See your anxiety as excitement. Break through negative stress, which is distress, into freedom."

The Now Experience

Sit in a chair that fits your body. Do not use a chair that is so big you curl up in it as a child or can't touch the floor with your feet. Nor one

Stress Can Be Managed

Hebble

"I'm so tired
I can't go on."

Hebble

"You stay out of that
mud, or I'll give you
a spanking you
won't forget!"

Hebble

"I don't have to scream
like my mother. There must
be a healthier way."

that is so small you feel like a grown-up trying to fit into a kindergarten chair when visiting a school.

Put your feet on the floor, uncross your arms, have your chin parallel with the floor (not tipped), and use the sentence "Now I am aware . . ." repeatedly as you become aware of your body and your senses.

Stay in this position. Select a current problem to think about. Observe yourself as you think.

The New Parent and Stress Reduction

The reduction of stress has become a major focus to those who are interested in a holistic approach to life. An overload of stress is seen as physically and emotionally destructive to a person. It is also destructive to interpersonal relationships.

Breaking free from the past and developing a new parent *now*, that is valuable *now*, and will be valuable in the future does not need to be *hard* work. It's OK if it's *easy* work, enjoyable work, successful work. It does not have to be agony. Agony increases stress in negative ways. Joy also increases stress yet does so in ways that most people want more of.

For more joy, the new inner parent needs to be potent, capable of providing protection, and willing to give you permission or encouragement to break free.

Potency in a new Parent can include many things. The most important is for the new Parent to be stronger in protective ways than the old parents might have been in negative ways. To become more potent the new Parent needs to be exercised frequently. The inner Child needs to defer to the new parent message. Yet children are often stronger than their parents and capable of controlling them. To avoid this possibility the rational, thinking Adult needs to take sides with the new Parent, to support the decisions and new positive messages. If the new Parent and the Adult function as a team, the inner Child will have its basic needs met and will feel a sense of *security*.

Protectiveness in a new Parent is also required for stress reduction. As people change, the monsters within often battle in favor of the way things used to be. While making changes, most people need to feel protected. Again, a Parent and Adult team can provide the strongest protection so that the inner Child will not only feel safe, it will feel as if it *belongs* and is loved.

Permission and encouragement in a new Parent are the new nurturing messages that break the old childhood spells and help set the person free. The messages encourage autonomous behavior rather than compulsive, driving behavior. Again, to find the right messages—the most effective messages—the team approach is preferred. Listening closely to what the inner Child needs and wants is a necessary step. So too is evaluating the needs and wants with the purpose of reducing negative stress.

Notes from a Workshop

Patricia, who had just lost her boyfriend, maintained her stress by not letting go. "I need freedom from old memories because they hurt too much. I *know* boyfriends come and go, but I've lost an important part of my life now that Steve has gone. What holds me like a ball and chain is feeling that everything with Steve was a horrible mistake and that maybe the relationship damaged my personality in some way.

"I know I exaggerate Steve's importance but I'm so anxious. I just worry all the time! Maybe I'll never meet another man, I say to myself, and I feel dumb because I'm so anxious, and I feel ugly 'cause Steve left. Then I don't do what I want to do and I don't take care of my body. I eat too much and sit around and don't exercise.

"Steve left me when I was down and out, and I believe if someone really loved me, they would stick with me through hard times. Steve's love wasn't mature. It was more like teenage infatuation because he only 'loved' me when I looked good and felt good.

"Now I want to stop thinking about him. It's causing me too much stress. I want to get some of my needs met *now* and not stay stuck thinking about the past or worrying about getting a boyfriend in the future."

One of the reasons Patricia had continued to recycle unpleasant memories was because she had had a mother who did the same. She constantly verbalized her opinions—over and over again. Weather, friends, and family were her favorite subjects. In discussing them so exhaustively her mother did not break free in her own life but stayed stuck and in continuing stress about unimportant issues. She was, of course, Patricia's model.

Patricia finally developed a new kind of parent, one who set reasonable limits on how long to grieve and feel bad. If distraught by something of minor importance, the new internal parent would say, "There, there, feel as bad as you want for twenty minutes, then get going." If upset by something of major importance, the new parent would say, "Honey, I know you feel really sad or mad. It's OK; after a while you'll begin to feel better and be able to put it out of your mind. So live now!"

Certainly these kinds of new parent messages would not fit everyone else, yet they illustrate what can be done to reduce the stress of compulsive thinking, to break free with new life.

Breakthrough V—The Needs of the Child

In this breakthrough you will discover that what people want may not be what they need—for example, wanting a lot of sweets but not needing them. Sometimes needs and wants coincide, like when we need to sleep and want to do so. Sometimes needs and wants don't coincide, like needing to sleep but wanting to stay awake.

Dialogue with the Child   During this stage of self-reparenting, it is necessary for your Adult to act as a good, nurturing parent to your Child and to elicit specific information while withholding all judgment. This exercise is for you to discover what your inner Child still needs or wants.

To make this discovery, first find a quiet place. Get in a comfortable position. Let your eyelids drop; let your body go limp.

Imagine you—as a child—sitting beside you as a grown-up. See yourselves in a pleasant situation such as sitting on a bench in a quiet park surrounded by flowers, or at the seashore where the sun is pleasant and the surf is quiet, or in the woods or mountains where the air is fresh and the sounds and smells are natural, or wherever else you enjoy going in your fantasy.

Speak internally to the little you, using a tender, loving, supportive voice and manner.

Use an endearing term or affectionate name or nickname as a parent might with a child.

Ask yourself:

"What do you want [endearing term such as 'honey']?"

"What do you need [endearing term]?"

Listen for your inner Child answers.

Encourage the inner dialogue.

Withhold all judgment at this time on whether what you want and need is good for you or not.

Just continue to use the two questions several times and listen to the answers.

Remember, good parents listen well.

Now list your Child's wants and needs below:

My Child Needs	*My Child Wants*

Evaluating with the Adult   Your Adult next needs to think about how the wants and needs of your Child can be met. When you evaluate, maintain a tender attitude, not an indulgent one. It is seldom good for children to have everything they want.

Look back at the preceding worksheet and star those items that seem most important. Give them a priority rating. Any item in both the wants and needs list is of high priority.

My Child's Wants and Needs	*What I Could Do about My Needs and Wants*	*What Others Could Do about My Needs and Wants*

Potency, Protection, and Permission   On the basis of the dialogue with your Child and your awareness of what you and others could do, design new parental statements to further your breaking free.

Potent statements my new Parent needs to make to my Child are:

Protections my new Parent needs to provide for my Child are:

Permissions and encouragements my new Parent needs to give my Child are:

Record your insights, especially your feelings, in your journal.

Sources
of Power

*"All power is a trust and we are accountable for its
exercise."*
   Disraeli

Many people experience a deep longing to change something about themselves or their situations. The longing to change indicates a basic hope that
change is possible. Typical statements made by people who believe in
change are: "Things are going to get better if I just give them a little time,"
or "I can change myself if I put my mind to it," or "If I change my goals, I
can get a better job." People who do not believe in change say things such
as, "Nothing will ever change" or "I feel helpless to change anything."

Whenever change is involved, some form of power is used. Physical power,
emotional power, intellectual power, and spiritual power may be used
singly or combined in some way to promote change.

In the last chapter you became more aware of what you need and want. In
this chapter you will learn more about your own sources of power and how
you can use them to help shape change in your life.

Expressions of Power

Power is a basic force of the universe. The sun and the moon have power, as
do the wind and the rain. The power of gravity is so important it keeps our
feet on the ground. Even the stars have power, and many people demon-

Power can Destroy

National Archives

"War starts."

National Archives

"War finishes."

National Archives

"War can start again."

strate the belief in this when they say, "Wish upon a star." Some form of power is expressed actively or is latent in every object, every situation, every person—at all times and in all places.

Power can be internal or external, individual or collective. People have power, ideas have power, even symbols are powerful. For example, a wedding ring symbolizes marriage; some people think it has the "power" to keep others away who might be attracted to the person wearing it. To others the ring symbolizes ownership by a spouse. The owner and the owned are linked through a symbol. Sometimes the symbol has only a legal connotation; sometimes it is a declaration of love and loyalty.

Human power is force or energy that may be used or stored up. People are born with power. They acquire more throughout life. They lose it all only at the time of death. The possession of power implies the inherent ability to use it—to change oneself, others, or the environment.

Many people have been told that power corrupts and absolute power corrupts absolutely yet have not thought of themselves as corrupt or corruptible. When something is corrupt, it is tainted, changed from good to bad.

Corruption can be found wherever people meet people, in political, social, and economic arenas. Less obvious are the everyday personal corruptions of power. Some of these are so common that references to them have become clichés. When people "drive like a maniac," "drink like a fish," or "eat like a pig," they are seldom considered corrupt in the same way a dictator or government might be thus labeled. Instead they are likely to be considered weak and with little willpower.

The use of power can be unhealthy or healthy. When unhealthy it is based on the desire to control others, to force them directly or through manipulation into conformity and obedience. When healthy it is used to encourage others in their growth toward self-mastery and self-actualization. The healthy use of personal power comes from the inner core of a person. It involves the flow of energy throughout that person.

Power and Your Child

Sit down and let yourself relax so that past memories emerge. Then start an inner dialogue. Let your Adult ask your Child the questions, "What powers did you have when you were little?" and "What powers did you want when you were little?"

Listen to the answers. Do they give you insight as to how learned to use or misuse power as a grown-up?

The Loss of Power

People often lose the sense of being alive and well—being vital—when they misuse or abuse the power they have. Suddenly they feel their energy is blocked and say something like, "I can't move, I feel so blocked inside," or "Everything new that I want to try on the job is blocked by some rule or procedure."

Another way people experience a loss of energy and power is when they are drained or burned out. When they feel this way, they may say, "I feel like a chicken without a head. I don't know who I am or where I'm going," or "I have five more things to do in five minutes," or "The phone rang all day. I'm washed out," or "I'm so exhausted I can't respond."

A third way people sense lowered vitality is when they are overly anxious or continually anxious. Whether the anxiety is rational or not, it creates stress. One of the ways a person's body responds to stress is by constriction. The Latin word for anxiety is *angustin,* which means "narrowness."

When people lose their vitality and power from either internal or external causes, they often experience a loss of self. In some cases, they "forget" who they are, where they live, and what values they live by. In other cases they may know their names and addresses, even the values they have had, yet they cease caring. They become depressed. "My life no longer has meaning," they may say, or "I don't like myself any more." The loss of vitality is always a sign that a person's needs are not being met.

If energy is visualized as a fast-moving river, then the way its energy can be blocked is with a dam, diverted by irrigation ditches or canals, or narrowed by impediments falling from the banks.

The same process applies to people. Laws, like dams, may block the expression of energy and vitality. Too many demands or requests may drain them dry. Exaggeration of their problems, complications, and unforeseen accidents may drop "debris" into their free-flowing channels. Anxiety may build, and freedom to be oneself setting one's own goals and directions seems to be a myth rather than a possibility.

Some of the common external sources of decreased vitality are: crowds, loud noise, criticism, isolation, lack of safety, poor food, unpleasant surroundings, uncomfortable clothes, exhausting life-styles, hot and humid weather, cold and windy weather, dirt, disorder, and pollution. Some of the common internal sources of decreased vitality are: preoccupation with mistakes, lack of self-esteem, depression, guilt, anger, confusion, fear, worry, and obsessions.

Energy Loss

Imagine a strong river moving swiftly to its destination. Then imagine how the energy flow is interrupted by a dam, by irrigation ditches, or by the banks caving in and thus narrowing the river's channel.

In the diagram shown here, record the customs or laws that *block* your energy like a dam, the time commitments and responsibilities that *drain* your energy like irrigation ditches, the anxiousness that narrows and *constricts* your energy.

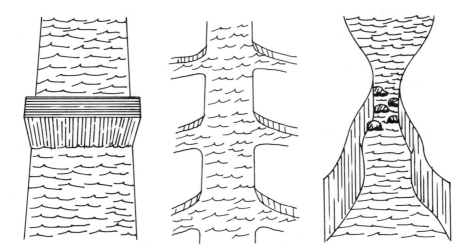

When your energy is blocked, drained off, or constricted, what do you do then?

Notes from a Workshop

Martin expressed the feeling of powerlessness he had when he was young and talked about how that affects his life now. "I had two older brothers, and they were so mean you wouldn't believe what they'd do to me. My mother and father both worked nights, and I'd be at the mercy of my brothers—no protection. They'd work me over physically in ways that didn't show and didn't leave bruises often, but the ways they hurt me were incredibly bad."

"I tried to tell my folks and they wouldn't listen. They'd just yell at me, 'Shut up. Don't make up stories.' Then they'd go back to their beer and TV. I tried to tell my third-grade teacher. She said I was a crybaby. Now I *won't* cry no matter what, but I have terrible nightmares and wake up cold and clammy and so weak. Sometimes when I even see men who remind me of my brothers, I feel weak again and at the same time feel rage. When I feel rage I feel powerful and almost welcome the feeling—right or wrong."

Vitality and Physical Power

Vitality is the foundation of personal power. The word *vital* comes from the Latin word *vita*, meaning life. To be alive is to be vital and know it—not intellectually but at the deepest level of being. Persons with high vitality often express a sense of liveliness and spontaneity. Though sometimes afraid, they feel as if they have the power to change. This vitality is positive and is often contagious.

However vitality can also be expressed negatively by people who are continually interested in others yet ignore their own needs. Such people tend to think of themselves as strong and caring and feel guilty if they want nurturing for themselves. After ignoring themselves for years, these people are likely to become physically ill. Sometimes their illness is like a blessing in disguise. At last they can start to take care of themselves. Or at last they will allow someone else to take care of them.

At an emotional level, people who ignore their own needs may suddenly break out in tears or suddenly start to complain, "I can't do another thing," or start to say "no" when before they've always said "yes," or make radical changes in their life-styles, sometimes even leaving their families or jobs. Yet each of these changes is a sign that the inner Child is struggling for some kind of freedom.

Low Vitality and the Loss of Energy

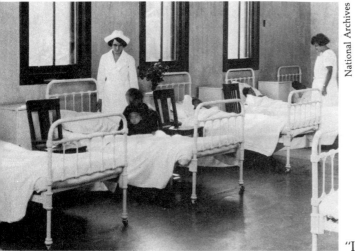

National Archives

"It's so lonesome here."

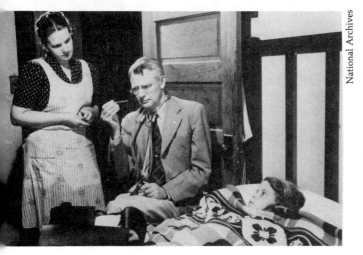

National Archives

"This could be serious."

"I've no energy left."

Hebble

When peoples' energy drops and they have less vitality, the old negative feelings in the Child ego state are often reexperienced. Feeling unwell physically is a common prelude to feeling unwell emotionally. At that time childhood tapes are often replayed. Common ones are "I'm not important" or "Nobody cares" or "I can't trust anyone to take care of me" or "I'll never make it." The Parent ego state may also become active when a person is ill and start an inner dialogue with the Child with comments such as:

"If you'd done what I told you, you wouldn't be sick."

"You're just lazy and pretending to be sick."

"Don't worry. Someone else can finish it."

"You need to take care of yourself, honey."

On the other hand the Adult ego state may get into the action. Running a high temperature, a person may respond logically from the Adult and go to bed or may also respond from the Adult and seek help from a physician.

All three ego states are capable of being activated at any time. The sense of vitality and health, or the lack of it, is most likely to be experienced by the Child. The sense of potent protection, "permission" and help in getting well, is most likely to come from a nurturing parent—either internal or external. Reparenting for many people requires them to create a new nurturing parent to put in their Parent ego state. This new parent can then function automatically, in nurturing ways, if they become ill.

Childhood Illness

Recall times in your childhood when you were injured or ill. Did your parents, or parent figures, treat you by using folklore remedies, traditional practices, or up-to-date procedures? Were they nurturing, indifferent, or annoyed at your physical condition? How did other people, such as siblings, respond?

What did you do when injured or ill? How did you feel? Did you take care of yourself or seek help from others? Did you accept your condition and focus on getting well? Did you fight it or ignore it in the hope that it would go away?

How do your childhood experiences affect your life now? Do you need to program your inner new Parent in some way to help you break out of negative habits?

Vitality in Spite of . . .

The positive use of vitality is related to wellness. Through improved diet and exercise, more and more people are concerned with high-level wellness. However, the sense of vitality and wholeness is not always lost when a person's physical body is handicapped in some way. In spite of poor health or physical handicaps, some people remain vital, loving, and alive.

Elizabeth Barrett Browning, an invalid in a wheelchair, wrote poetry, and Henri Matisse, when he could no longer hold his paintbrushes to paint, created new art with collages of bits of colored paper. Paraplegics can play sports from their wheelchairs and support themselves financially. And those who have problems such as cerebral palsy, epilepsy, blindness, or some other crippling disease learn how to develop compensating positive skills and adapt.

Whole people, whether physically handicapped or not, know that they live in their bodies. They do not deny them. They treat them with respect, not abuse. They also know that they are more than machines that think; they know the way they use their minds is related to education, life experiences, capacities to think and reason, and to their sense of bodily well-being, their courage, and their search for freedom. The spirit that they exhibit often compensates for the health they have "lost."

The Power of Personality

When people are described as having a strong spirit or a powerful personality, it is usually because a particular use of power is very evident and reflects the intensity of the energy from one of the ego states. Controlling and nurturing power comes from the Parent ego state, intellectual power comes from the Adult ego state, rebellious competitive power, compliant and adapted power, comes from the Child; so does natural power. The use of natural power begins even before the event of birth.

Controlling power often enslaves others. If used as a punishing power, it is destructive. The brutalizing of women and children, the killing of one person by another, are the most common examples of the punishing power of others. Any form of physical force and violence or the extension of force with the use of weapons is controlling. In a less extreme form, people often use critical or sarcastic words or facial expressions to punish and control others.

Furthermore, people use punishing power on themselves. They might force their bodies beyond physical limits, ignore their bodily needs, or mistreat themselves. They might pull out their eyelashes or bite their fingers. They might overeat or overdrink and thus hurt themselves so that later they can punish themselves and feel guilty. If they experience low self-esteem or guilt, they might seek job situations, spouses, or friends who will use punishing power on them. The sadomasochistic dimension in their lives keeps them enslaved. "I hate myself" or "I hate others" is the basic orientation of a punishing, controlling person.

In the process of self-reparenting, the difference between punishing and controlling needs to be clear. Most people have had enough punishment, from themselves and from others. They don't need any more. Many people, however, need to learn self-control and are likely to need a firm, loving parent who will set limits for them.

Nurturing power is power used on behalf of a person, as when teaching or caring or encouraging those who need care. Most people need to be more nurturing to themselves in healthy ways. When they are, the nurturing shows through. They are physically attractive at any age in life. They care for their bodies and it shows in how they eat, how they sleep, how they exercise, and how they pace themselves with rest and recreation. The use of nurturing power on others encourages their growth; the use of nurturing power on oneself encourages self-actualization. "I like myself" and "I can take care of myself and others" is the basic orientation.

Some people confuse nurturing with overindulgence. When overindulgent with themselves, they will not set limits. They easily give in to their Child's desires, whether the desires are healthy ones or not. They may allow themselves to go on eating, drinking, or buying binges. If people have an overindulgent Parent, their inner Child is likely to feel fearful (because no limits are set) or become narcissistic (believing they are "entitled" to everything they desire, including unlimited approval from others).

A different pattern is observable in people who are very nurturing to others and very punishing to themselves. They are like this usually because they were trained as children to take care of others and told that it was "selfish" to focus on themselves. As grown-ups they often feel guilty if they put themselves first and uncomfortable unless they are taking care of others. They listen to their internal jailer rather than figure out how to get free.

Competitive power can be negative or positive. In sports, competition can be positive—if it is fair. So too in the professional and business world. However, taking an unfair advantage and not playing by the rules is negative competitive power. It is expressed by people who want to win, "by fair means or foul."

Competitive power is most noticeable in interpersonal situations where physical vitality or intellectual strength is often used. "I want to be first and most important" is the basic orientation of highly competitive persons.

In many families, people experience both power and powerlessness. Parents may feel powerful or helpless in directing their children. The children may feel the same about their parents. All too often competing for power becomes a family game.

During the process of self-reparenting, an inner battle may rage within, between the Parent and the Child, much like the family battles in childhood. In such cases the urge to break free and create something new—a new self—may be throttled by conflict and competition with oneself. When this occurs, another source of power needs to be activated—the Adult.

A person's Adult can act as a referee between the Parent and Child and redirect the energy toward dynamic growth and against the negative power forces, internal or external, that interfere with freedom. This use of competitive power is noticeable in people who strive for competence, who want to do their best, who set goals that contribute to self-actualization and to the rights of all people to freedom and the pursuit of happiness. Competitive power is also valuable when people respect each other and "argue things through" to a new synthesis and truth.

Analytical power is the power of the Adult ego state to discern, to collect information, to sort out what is important and what is not, to use and discard relevant and irrelevant information. When using their analytical power, people take the feelings in their inner Child into consideration. They recognize that they can be in charge of their own feelings. They have the feelings; the feelings do not have them. Consequently they do not allow their feelings to flood them so that they are incapable of thinking.

They are also aware of the traditions and prejudices of their own national and family cultures and how these are passed on, generation after generation, through the Parent ego state. With analytical power they consider whether their beliefs from the past are still appropriate.

As one woman reported, "When I was a little girl I lived on a farm and rode horses a lot. So did my mom and dad, and I loved the wind on my face and feeling free. It was part of our family tradition. I still daydream about having a horse, but here in San Francisco, when I analyze the situation, I know it's just not practical."

Adapted power is the natural power of a child that has been adapted by parents, peers, and situations. Much as a generator converts one form of power to another, training and various traumas convert one form of a child's power to another. Compliance to authorities and defiance by procrastinating or rebelling are the most common adaptive styles that are learned in childhood and may or may not lead to freedom.

Adapted power can be negative or positive. For example, some persons' natural healing powers become so blocked that they adapt to a life of illness. Some children experience so much brutality that they adapt to a life of fear and mistrust.

More positive examples are children who adapt themselves to school and learn to study, or who adapt some of their inclinations of carelessness to the mores of cleanliness and courtesy. The first forms of adaptation often give people a sense of intellectual power; the second gives them some power to feel socially acceptable.

Creative power is the capacity to develop new ideas, new objects, new lifestyles. With the use of creative power people can find nonviolent ways to solve conflicts, to create art, to imagine the possibility and the effects of change. The source of this power is in the Child ego state and is likely to be highest when a person feels alive and well.

Imagination is one of the most potent creative powers that all people have. It can be used in positive or negative ways. Using the power to imagine—to image something new—people can design machinery for destruction and machinery for physical diagnosis and healing. Both emerge from the human power to create something new.

Natural power is power experienced at the most basic physical level. It is the power people are naturally born with, the power that keeps them alive. It is the power of the body to move, to breathe, to eat, to sleep, to see, to taste, to feel, to hear. It is that magnificent power to be. It is the power that is the source of our vitality and, in some forms, is experienced even before birth.

If this natural power is lost, death comes. If this natural power is radically decreased or blocked in some way, the power of a new nurturing, encouraging parent is needed.

Notes from a Workshop

Sidney was a competent corporation vice-president who barely avoided a physical and emotional collapse. He reported the process:

"It's incredible the way I used to treat myself. I used to drive myself so hard that every night I would fall into bed totally exhausted. I did this for years.

"Then I slowly became aware that I was burning myself out. My pep and vitality were gone. I lost my creativity and my power to think analytically. I didn't want any more responsibility for my kids or staff. I couldn't meet the quotas set for me by the company. It seems like I had lost all my natural power.

"For two weeks, I just withdrew. I stayed in bed most of the time and wouldn't even talk to the family. Then I began to realize that the slave driver was me—not my wife, not my boss. "That's why I'm here. Somebody said I needed to learn how to be a good parent to myself so I could get back the power that I lost."

This unhealthy competitive attitude was also expressed by Carol, a woman whose husband had just moved out:

"I'm here because I always feel out of place with people unless I'm competing. I'm a good tennis player and usually win. I want to have the highest grades in the college classes I'm taking and get really jealous if someone else is as good or better. At parties I want to be the best dressed, and of course I want my children to be best at school. Now my husband is mad and wants a divorce, and he says that all I want is to win—win in arguments with him, which we have every day. Suddenly I feel like I'm going to fall apart. My daddy used to tell me that the most important thing in life was winning. Now here I am losing. I feel like I'm breaking up in little pieces."

A Source of Power

Sit down in an easy chair. Let your body relax. Let your body really relax, not curled up or crunched over but in relatively straight lines.

Now imagine you see a flower, a bush, or a tree growing yet struggling in arid soil, without enough water or other nutrients. In your imagination look at it closely. Where is it getting its power to grow?

Now imagine the same flower, bush, or tree in rich soil where the water is adequate and the needed nutrients are available. How is the picture different?

Now see yourself as though you were a flower, a bush, or a tree. What is the aridness you grew up in? What is the richness? How has each affected your growth?

The Power of Thinking

In today's culture there is such a strong emphasis on getting in touch with one's feelings that the capacity to think is often taken for granted. Yet people who think usually have more power than those who don't. Being able to think clearly and creatively is necessary for freedom and autonomy.

Jean Piaget, the Swiss psychologist, popularized the phrase *cognitive development* to refer to the way people learn to think. He was more interested in how they think than in how they feel. He wanted to discover how people acquire knowledge through perception, intuition, reasoning, and information and developed his theory by careful, systematic hour-by-hour observation of children, including his own. Piaget discovered that as with physical development, cognitive development progresses in four stages or phases, with plateaus in between.

Each of the four major stages is a system of learning how to think and is different from other stages. These stages occur in sequence. Therefore, before moving from one to the next, children need to have sufficient experience with the one they are on.

The first stage or system of thinking develops from birth to two years old. At this time the cognitive development of children is largely through their senses and their experiences. Without understanding their parents' words, they learn whether it is safe to trust their parents. Without words of their own to explain needs and wants, they still get their messages across. A yell, a smile, a face full of tears are appeals for immediate gratification. At this age, children learn to play games such as peek-a-boo. They remember family members who leave their sight temporarily and become frantic in a search for a favorite teddy bear or blanket. They "trust" that certain authorities will come and take care of them. When this trust is badly shaken, normal development may be upset, and children may begin to stop thinking. They may act confused or select one of the three basic ways of adapting: obedience, rebellion, or procrastination.

The next stage of learning how to think occurs from ages two to seven years old. At the beginning of this stage, children do not understand that certain ways of operating lead to certain results. Freely they use their natural intuitiveness, which is often right. Freely they think in ways that may seem illogical to those who are older. "No" and "Why?" are often responses to parental demands. At this age children enjoy talking to themselves just to hear themselves talk. Of course many grown-ups also talk to themselves. Children, however, are aware that they are doing it and they enjoy doing it. Grown-ups, when they become aware that they are talking to themselves, are more likely to feel embarrassed.

Language development is rapid during these years. The average two-hundred-word vocabulary of a two year old jumps to an average of two thousand words by the age of five. Along with this comes a rich fantasy life. These two aspects of learning language and fantasy can lead to a sense of new freedom. These fantasies of childhood years, whether negative or positive, may become the script for a lifetime.

Between ages seven and eleven, children begin to reason out solutions to problems. They understand concrete or specific parts of a problem and are capable of learning many skills. At this age they become very literal-minded. As an example, when I was getting close to the end of a pregnancy, I laughingly commented to one of my sons, "I'm getting so fat the baby will pop right out of my ears." For days he observed me curiously, then asked from a literal perspective: "How can a baby get out that little hole in your ear?"

Children in this stage often know the difference between facts and dreams although not between fact and theory. Once they decide "that's the way it is," they often refuse to change their opinion, regardless of new facts. Of course, many people much older may be like this. They may have turned off their earlier capacity to be intuitive. They may listen only to words and not pick up on important nonverbal messages. Consequently they tend to be rigid rather than flexible in their thinking.

The fourth step in learning to think occurs in children from eleven to sixteen years. At this age they are able to think more rationally (although they may not do so). For the first time they are developmentally able to think abstractly, though they may not do so. They are able to think beyond the immediate here-and-now and begin to form theories about many things. Once again they grapple with the lifelong questions of "Who am I?" and "What am I doing here?"

People who go through each cognitive stage of development and do not get stuck en route have more free choices than do the ones who are imprisoned in their adaptations. They are able to comply if they decide they want to. They can also rebel or procrastinate if that is their choice. The point is, they are able to think and act freely, not compulsively.

Each of these types of people with their predictable patterns of response needs a new parent who will encourage them to think clearly on the basis of current facts. Thinking clearly, instead of nonthinking or confused thinking on the basis of childhood experiences, is a major road to freedom.

Sometimes freedom will mean going against authorities and peers who may say things such as:

Learning Is Energizing

National Archives

"This is interesting."

Pearson

"I know the answer."

"It's never too late to graduate."

James

"Do what you feel like doing without thinking so much."

"Lose your mind and come to your senses."

"Follow your feelings, not your reason."

"Stop thinking all the time."

Thinking clearly requires decontaminating the logical, rational Adult ego state from outdated prejudices and unrealistic fears of the past. This is possible because with the Adult, a person can ask questions such as, "Am I in touch with all my sources of power?" "Am I using all my powers?" "Or am I draining myself dry? Or blocking my energy in some way? Or giving in to unnecessary anxiety?"

Thinking about questions like these often expands the horizon much like the questions presented at the beginning of the book: "Who am I?" "What am I doing with my power? Am I using it to break free?"

Thinking and Problem Solving

When you think about how you think, what do you think? Do you trust your current thinking process?

Do you ever feel stuck—as if there is some kind of skill or information that you haven't learned that would make life easier for you if you did learn it?

Do you ever feel confused, as if you were pushed ahead in school when not quite ready for it? If so, at what stage of cognitive development?

Do you solve problems by thinking in the ways you were taught to think? Do you solve problems by thinking the opposite of what you were taught to think? Do you solve problems by not thinking? Just waiting for them to go away?

Do you need to reparent yourself with a phrase such as "It's OK to go back to school" or "It's OK to think clearly"?

Spiritual Power

Historically people have often been described in terms of body, mind, and spirit. Yet since the discovery of modern psychology the concept of the spirit has been widely discarded, ignored, or denied in Western culture. This is beginning to change, largely due to Eastern influences on Western thought; a holistic approach is the new focus.

The word *health* comes from the Anglo-Saxon root *hal,* which means both "whole" and "holy." Holistic techniques often focus on self-management, awareness and strengthening one's own body with the use of massage, exercise, relaxation, proper nutrition and the balancing of energy, awareness of psychological problems and learning how to solve them, and awareness of the spiritual dimension of existence.

Persons who are whole experience a sense of harmony. Their bodies, minds, and spirits tend toward integration as well as individuation. Yet spiritual power may be active even in people who have problems and lack wholeness. For example, people who are faced with sure death or loss of freedom often experience spiritual power. Other people who are limited in their intellectual or social development may not make competent decisions or develop authentic relationships. Yet they too may experience the power of the spirit.

For many centuries people have searched for words to describe the concept "spiritual." The Egyptians used the word *Ka* to denote the transcendent part of a person, that which is neither mind nor body. The Hebrews used *nephesh,* meaning "breath." The Greeks used the word *psyche,* which can be translated as "soul" or "mind." It may be part of our DNA structure. Whatever it is, it functions with high autonomy in complex ways.

The world spirit refers to the vital animating force in a person, which can also move that person beyond the normal confines of this world into transcendent moments when wholeness and holiness are experienced. These moments are peak experiences, seemingly outside of normal categories of time and space. They are possible because of the power of the spirit and its liberating effect on persons. Peak experiences can be moments when everything seems one—body, mind, and spirit. Or when one seems one with others and with God or experiences a cosmic awareness of being part of the universe, which is perceived as an integrated and unified whole. It is a moment of indescribable clarity.

Although some philosophies deny the existence of a spiritual component in human beings, there is today a ground swell to recognize the spiritual part of a person, even if this element is not easily defined or readily understood. For me, the spiritual part of the self is a reality, the inner core of a person's being. It is capable of transcendence in many forms. Perhaps it is immortal. It is surely the essence of a person.

Today increasing numbers of people are becoming aware of how they have ignored or denied and thus been alienated from the source of spiritual power. They are finding out that they have not listened to the spirit within or trusted the "inner light" or committed themselves to a larger universal order, and they are searching for it in many ways. People are turning to meditation, prayer, parapsychology, and holistic health to get in touch with their inner selves and with the peace and power that often accompanies that process.

Because of spiritual power, a person may be said to have a spiritual self, as well as a biological and psychological self. This spiritual self does not need to be described in theological terms, although many may choose to do so.

The belief in the spirit is often accompanied by the belief that the human spirit is connected to an external power or a reflection of it. Some call this power "God." Others speak of this force as Truth, Light, Tao, Christ, Allah, Jehovah, Atman, Siva, Buddha, Life Energy, Cosmic Power—or use words with similar or different spiritual connotations. In the incredibly popular movie *Star Wars*, it is merely called "the Force" and is pitted against the powers of evil personified by Darth Vadar.

Just because many people believe in spiritual power is not proof that it exists. Just because many people do *not* believe in it also is no proof. What does seem clear is that even if spiritual power is denied or deprecated by some, it doesn't go away. It is free energy, not bound by human limitations.

Transcendent Experiences

Recall times when for a brief period you were caught up in a moment of transcendence.

How did you explain it to yourself?

Did you use theological or philosophical concepts or something else?

What effect have these spiritual experiences had on increasing the freedom in your life?

A Personal Note

I remember once when I was caught up in ecstasy on hearing what poets have called "the music of the spheres." It was very early in the morning. The sky was still dark. The day before I had experienced another breakthrough to freedom by giving up some old negative beliefs that were interfering with satisfaction and enjoyment of life. I was outside, sitting on a little wooden bench that faced east, wondering what this new freedom would mean in my life.

Slowly the sun began to rise over the low mountains ahead. Slowly the rays spread out and the colors changed. The dewdrops on the leaves glistened like diamonds. One star still shone at a distance. A rooster crowed, and close at hand a bird welcomed the day. Suddenly there was an outburst of music in my being—music I had never heard or could imagine hearing. It was music that carried me beyond time and space. I *know* I heard it. I *know* it was the music of the spheres. That moment never came again, yet it changed my life permanently. The fear of inevitable death left me. It never returned, even when on two occasions imminent death seemed probable. The experience affected me in another important way. At last I knew the courage to be. At last I could affirm, "I am who I am." Now, some years later, I still long for the joy of that particular moment and the transcendence that was briefly mine.

Breakthrough VI—You and Your Power

You already have a great deal of power. The purpose of this section is to assist you to break through to freedom with more awareness of the power you have to do it.

Vitality for a New Life: Go back to your childhood and recall times when you felt a sense of high vitality and fill in the following:

I was about _____ years old and I was in the following situation

_____.

I think the vitality I experienced there was related to _____

_____.

It felt good because _____.

If I want to feel that way more often, I need to _____

instead of _____

which I now do. Then I will be living my new life.

Use and Misuse of Power: Think of the following categories and record how you use and misuse each of the powers of your personality.

Types of power	How I use it	How I misuse it
Punishing power:		
Nurturing power:		
Competitive power:		
Analytical power:		
Adapted power:		
Creative power:		
Natural power:		

Are the ways you use and misuse your powers similar to the way your parents dealt with their powers?

If something more needed in your new Parent ego state? If so, how can you use your Adult to restructure it? Don't be helpless and powerless. Think. What do you need to do?

Reparenting Your Powers: The powers you have and use are partially the result of the ways you were parented and partially a result of other factors in your life.

List the strong powers you are already aware of having and the weaker powers you need to strengthen.

	Power I Have	*Power I Need to Develop*
Physical powers		
Personality powers		
Thinking powers		
Spiritual powers		

As you look at your list, ask yourself what encouraging messages you need from your new developing Parent so that you can strengthen your powers that are weak. Make a list of what you need to do and say to yourself.

Now record any new insights you might have in your journal.

Creating
Strengths

7

It's as hard to see oneself as to look backwards without turning around.
   Henry David Thoreau

In spite of the difficulty in seeing oneself clearly, people have tried to do so since the beginning of time. With or without education, they have chosen creative ways of looking at themselves. Whether reading comic books, newspapers, novels, poetry, or nonfiction literature, watching television or movies, people have identified with the person or themes. They often see themselves in the creative acts of others. Viewing a great picture, some have said to themselves, "Yes, that's me," or "That's how I want to be," or "No, I'm not like that, or am I?" Listening to nostalgic or soul-moving music has stirred many peoples' emotions and led them to a deeper awareness of themselves. "Who am I?" and "Where am I going?" are questions for a lifetime.

Some people are not aware of the questions. Others don't care. Or if they care, they don't care about the answers. Some, with more concern for finding out who they are, want the answers but also want someone else to tell them the answers. A fourth and smaller group of people comprises those who are determined to seek the answers for themselves. They have will and purpose and they use these capacities in creative ways. If you've read this far in this book, you are a member of this last group.

This chapter will show you what it means to become an artist in creating a new parent for yourself. No doubt you have already come a long way in designing your new parent. However, you still may feel frustrated by your needs and the stresses of recognizing these needs and the blocks that are still in your way to breaking free.

The prerequisites to creativity, as well as the development of virtues such as hope, will, purpose, competence, fidelity, love, care, and wisdom, are included here. With them you can become an artist at reparenting yourself. If you are able to wish and want, hope and trust, you will find new competency and strength.

Prerequisites to Creativity

Becoming creative requires the capacity to wish, to want, and to will. Wishing, wanting, and willing do not necessarily lead to being creative. Yet without these qualities, creativity does not mature.

The capacity to wish is part of being human. It begins in early childhood, first with the wishing for physical comfort such as "I wish I was warm," or "I wish I had something to eat." It develops into wishing for people who can satisfy the need for comfort: "I wish Daddy would come home" or "I wish Mama would hold me." It next develops into a desire for things such as little red wagons and storybook dolls. Wishing is a necessary prelude to wanting.

When people want something, they often begin to set goals and mobilize their wills to reach their goals. Their desires become more intense and are often related to the immediate situation:

"I want to play outside."
"I want you to come inside this minute."
"Wah; I wanna play!"

The initial wish and the stronger feeling of wanting somebody or something is based on the capacity to hope which develops during infancy. Wishing is often part of a daydream. Not so, wanting. Wanting is more focused. It activates a person's will and the determination to make choices. Making choices is a continuing process in creating a new life.

Notes from a Workshop

Many events interfere with the development of wishing, wanting, and willing. Being abandoned, lied to, brutalized, or betrayed by parents or parental figures in early life, or by siblings or friends, are devastating experiences that leave scars on the psyche. Broken promises also interfere with daring to wish, daring to hope.

Norman, a computer programmer, explained how it happened to him:

> "I never knew what to expect. My dad would often promise things, like promising to take me to a ball game. Then he would be 'too busy' or 'too tired' or 'too something.' I finally learned not to count on him.

> "My mother was different but the same. She would promise, promise, promise not to lose her temper. Then the smallest thing would trigger her off. So I learned to keep away from her. When she got angry she acted crazy. Now I guess people think I'm a loner. I don't care what they think. I don't want anything any more. I've given up hope. Somebody said hope was an opiate. I think that's right. There's no point wishing for anything."

When Sally began therapy, her self-esteem was very low. The problem that she first wanted to talk about was her fear that her husband would leave. "I just don't trust him to stay around," she lamented. "I don't know why, but I feel very insecure. It's almost as if I *expect* to be left alone like I was so much of the time when I was little and my folks would go to the corner bar. I never knew if, or when, they would come back. They used to tell me that if I cried, they'd leave me for good. Then one day when I was very little my dad didn't return ever, and I kind of expect my husband to do the same. I just don't trust him."

Jeanette, also in the workshop, looked at her in amazement. "Well, I don't know why you feel so bad. At least they were alive! My mother died soon after I was born so I never really knew her. All I had was her picture, no real memories. My aunt brought me up. Of course, I know in my head it wasn't my mother's fault, but at the *feeling* level, I often feel hopeless. Furthermore, I don't seem to have any will power."

Roger interrupted, "Well, I grew up in an orphanage. So what! I find it best to just keep on working hard. Then I forget stuff like that, and I don't need to get close to people like all the books say you 'should' do." I've stopped wishing and wanting.

Learning to Wish

When you were a child, what did you wish for? What did you want?

How were you encouraged to express your wishes or deny them?

Your parents were your models for turning wishes into reality. Did your parents seem to live their own lives to get what they wished for?

If they did not, what do you suppose interfered?

Logical and Creative Thinking

People think in different ways, some more logical, some more creative than others. Logical, clear thinking is not the same as creative thinking. In some situations—such as balancing a checkbook—logical thinking is most appropriate. In other situations—such as when designing a gourmet dinner or a new program—creative thinking is more effective. Logic alone seldom leads to new ideas. When new ideas or new solutions are needed, logic and creativity together are most effective.

The clearest logical thinking comes from the Adult ego state. It develops as a result of going through the cognitive developmental stages often with parental encouragement. In contrast, creative thinking is encouraged by the free, nonadapted part of the Child ego state. Creative thinking usually involves the right hemisphere of the brain, which perceives things in visual holistic ways, while the left hemisphere specializes in logical and analytical thinking. An artist uses both hemispheres.

Today there is an increasing awareness of the value of integrating the right-brain and left-brain hemispheres, a strong indication that some people are more interested in learning how to think creatively than in reinforcing analytical ways of thinking. This is essential in breaking free.

One of the problems in the breakthrough to freedom is to look for various options like the Roman god Janus. Janus, the god for gates and doors for whm the month of January is named, is depicted on old Roman coins as guarding the gates by looking in two directins at the same time. Creative persons look both ways at once. They are lateral thinkers; they use their intuition; they let ideas develop. Ideas often come from hidden places. Awareness often comes with a synthesis of opposing ideas or polarities, or an extension of previous ideas.

A common pattern for creative people is to think intently about some issue, then focus their attention elsewhere while the unconscious mind does its work and brings new insight and solutions into consciousness.

Creative people often require solitude for hours or days at a time so that they can get in touch with their inner selves. At that time they may seem to "do nothing"; actually they may be daydreaming or brainstorming an idea. Brainstorming is allowing thoughts to go in any direction without the judgment or restraint that may be necessary at a later time.

The basis of creativity is freedom and the urge for newness. Creativity is possible because the developmental crises of childhood have been partially solved. The person has learned to trust and therefore hopes; has taken beginning steps toward autonomy and therefore has developed will; has resolved some of the issues of identity and therefore knows a sense of purpose; has achieved some successes and therefore feels competent to create.

Creativity is always possible. When it is repressed or stunted, a new parent is needed who can give "permission" to walk the freedom road. Developing a new parent is a creative act. Logical thinking is needed; so too is intuition.

The Value of Intuition

One of the tools for creative thinking is the use of intuition. Apparently this is a capacity that people are born with. Using their senses, they "intuit" whether a situation is warm, happy, and conducive to a growing freedom or whether it is restrictive, unhappy, and leading to a form of slavery.

Intuition is knowledge based on experience and acquired unconsciously or preconsciously. The dictionary defines it as "the quick perception of truth without conscious attention or reasoning." Some people trust their intuition more than their logical thinking and make comments such as:

> "I have a vague but intense feeling about the trip . . . "
>> "I have a hunch everything will turn out OK . . . "
>>> "I knew it was going to happen . . . "
>>>> "I sense you're anxious . . . "
>>>>> "I trust my hunches . . . "

Intuition is a natural creative power. It is often quashed by overadapting and staying stuck in the driver type of compulsive behavior. Many parents would rather have obedient children than creative ones because creative children often stir up a mess. Yet in spite of adaptations, the ability to use intuition remains a lifelong potential and people either learn to trust it or not. If they trust it, the inner Child uses intuition, knowingly or unknowingly, in creative ways.

If they do not trust this intuition, they may feel "stuck" with self-doubt and the lack of autonomy. Externally they may *appear* to be successful, moving ahead with will and purpose. Actually they are not free. They are merely following their old programmed patterns.

Your Intuition and Creativity

Think back over the past week or two when you knew, intuitively, that something was true but you didn't know how you knew.

What did you do next with that knowledge? Did you deny it? Did you put your intuition to work to service your creativity? If so, how? If not, what intervened?

What does your new parent need to say to you so that you can creatively expand your new life?

Vertical and Lateral Thinking

A different way to think about thinking is to compare "vertical" and "lateral" categories as developed by Edward DeBono. Vertical thinking follows the most obvious straight line, either up or down. It is logical. Lateral thinking does not follow the logical straight path. It jumps in search of new solutions to old problems in creative ways.

For example, some people, when trying to solve a problem, "keep hitting their heads against the wall." They do not explore creative options. They "try and try and try" and don't succeed. Yet DeBono wrote, people "cannot dig a hole in a different place by digging the same hole deeper. Vertical thinking digs the same hole deeper; lateral thinking is concerned with digging a hole in another place."

Vertical thinkers are somewhat like the seven- to eleven-year-old child who is literal-minded and reasonable. The Adult ego state is well formed at this age, although it may not have as much information stored in its computer as it will some years later.

In contrast, lateral thinkers also use the Adult but in cooperation with their creative Child. They allow their senses, experiences, and intuition, as well as their logical abilities, to show them where to "dig a hole in another place." Einstein, for example, created the theory of relativity not by vertical thinking but by lateral thinking; he looked at old information in new ways. He did not perform experiments that led to the theory. The experiments came after, as a way of proving the theory.

Lateral Thinking is Creative

"I'm creating a new plan for my life."

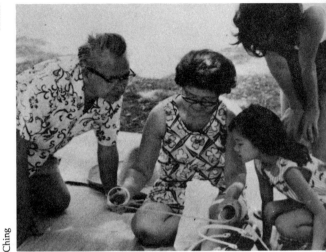

"We can figure out a new way to make it work."

"If we don't strike oil here we'll dig another hole."

A common cliché often used to discount creative thinking is, "There's nothing new under the sun." Maybe so, but there was a time in history when wheels had not yet been invented and then they were. That was new. It's hard to give up on a half-dug hole, a half-solved problem. It doesn't seem logical after so much effort, yet "hole hopping" is necessary for freedom. To be a one-hole digger is to be adapted to slavery and to be content with it.

Lateral Thinking for Problem Solving

List one of your recurring problems that you have tried to solve, maybe with vertical, one-hole thinking. One-hole thinking is digging deeper into the problem without looking at options. Where might you dig additional holes (solutions)? Think quickly, write quickly. Don't evaluate.

A problem I have: _____.

A solution I've tried: _____.

My fast list of other possible solutions: _____

_____.

Now ask yourself how you can continue to use lateral thinking for other problems.

Developmental Steps for Creating Strengths

Both kinds of thinking—logical and creative—are necessary in designing a new life. And becoming creative requires the development of certain virtues. The word *virtue* has a positive meaning. It refers to the human qualities of strength. Psychologist Erik Erikson believes the development of particular virtues or strengths occurs at specific age levels if people solve the basic conflicts associated with that age.

Although Erikson based his ideas on some of Freud's concepts, he also moved beyond them to define the crisis of each age. This part of his work is known to many. What is known to few is how the resolution of each age crisis leads to the development of specific virtues—hope, will, purpose,

The Wonder of Developing Strengths

James

"I wonder are you there?"

National Archives

"I wonder what it feels like."

National Archives

"I wonder if he can dance."

"I wonder what the birthday cake will be like."

James

milk
white bread
Trullo Seeves
trullee club ?

competence, fidelity, love, care, and wisdom. The development of these strengths depends upon the development of previous ones, and can be diagrammed in this way:

Age of Development	Developmental Crisis	Result If Crisis Is Solved
0–1½	Basic trust vs. mistrust	Hope
1½–3	Autonomy vs. shame and self-doubt	Will
3–7	Initiative vs. guilt	Purpose
7–12	Mastery vs. inferiority	Competence
12–18	Identity vs. identity confusion	Fidelity
18–30	Intimacy vs. isolation	Love
30–60	Generativity vs. stagnation	Care
Over 60	Ego integrity vs. despair	Wisdom

I believe that the "age of development" could be called "age of creativity" because each person needs creative ways to solve each problem, and "developmental crisis" could be renamed "creative challenges." I like the word *creative* because I think each step involves marshaling one's strengths to move on "in spite of . . ."

People with these strengths have solved some basic conflicts within themselves that are part of growing up, whether they were aware of them or not. When the conflicts are not solved, the problem keeps cropping up.

Many people do not resolve their developmental conflicts. They stay stuck. Therefore development of some of their potentials is thwarted. Usually it is because of the spells in childhood that interfered with the growth of creativity. When potentials are turned off, less creative energy is available to them for breaking through to freedom.

Trust versus mistrust: Infancy is a real crisis period for a child. To trust or not to trust, that is the question. The crisis is resolved if nurturing, warm, affectionate care is given and if the immediate environment and people are experienced as dependable.

To trust is to feel confidence in something or some person. The object or person is believed to be reliable. To discover trust means to gain knowledge of it in some way—by search, study, or personal experience. It is to find something or somebody who is trustworthy.

Unfortunately many people do not find what they are looking for or they lose what they do find. The feeling of trust falls into this category. Many never find it; many more lose it. Those who do not find it go through life feeling a gnawing sense of emptiness and powerlessness. Those who find it and lose it go through life feeling a gnawing sense of loneliness and power-lessness. The feelings may be like a high tide that almost sweeps them off their feet, or like a low tide that hardly moves within yet is experienced as constant depression.

A lack of trust not only creates depression. It may interfere with healthy de-velopment. Children who are ignored or seldom touched or starved do not mature at a normal rate. The emaciated bodies and look of terror in the eyes of children who suffer from the inhumanities of war provide some of the most tragic evidence that physical development, as well as social, intellec-tual, and moral development, may be interrupted, even stopped, at an early age.

Less noticeable and more common are those who are physically abused. This too can destroy the capacity to trust and hope. So does being aban-doned, whether due to death, divorce, or desertion. The lack of trust may be emotional, not rational (after all, many parents are not to "blame" for their deaths). Unknowingly the children may expect others to leave them in later life and because of this underlying fear may cling dependently to some-one or may act in ways to "force" the other person to leave.

Maternal deprivation is said to be the one factor that most interferes with the development of trust. Studies show that even with well-intentioned, competent substitute care, development may not be as rapid or complete. For example, an infant who becomes very ill and has to be hospitalized may, without awareness, learn to mistrust parents. They are perceived as deserters who do not come when they are called and do not comfort or re-move the pain and fear. Later in life, persons with this or similar experiences may have difficulty asking for what they want.

Hope is the virtue that results from the successful resolution of this conflict between whether or not it is safe to trust parents. Hope is the belief that certain wishes are attainable "in spite of . . ." More important than trust, hope can continue even when trust is shattered. If this dilemma is not resolved, a sense of mistrust and the accompanying hopelessness begins to grow. When people are hopeless, this may continue throughout a lifetime, covered up perhaps with a workaholic life-style or an unrealistic Pollyanna attitude.

Autonomy versus shame and self-doubt: The necessary dependence during the first year and a half of life begins to take a new direction as children, ages one and a half to three, become aware of their power to use their bodies. They discover they don't need to be carried. They can walk and do many things on their own. This is the beginning of autonomy; "I can do it" is the new experience, unless they are overly restricted to crib and playpen.

Children of this age often do not want to let mother out of sight, yet they want to be independent when she is around. Along with this comes some self-doubt—"I can't do it alone—and shame for not being able to be independent.

Shame is experienced as a diffused sense of anxiety, self-doubt as not living up to a fantasized ideal. Both feelings are based on a decision of "I am weak or inadequate." This is toilet-training time, so it is not surprising that shame is often described as feeling exposed—"caught with one's pants down."

If the conflicts are not resolved, and for many people they are not, then patterns of helplessness begin to surface. Self-doubt and fear of trying new experiences may plague these people throughout life. If the conflicts of this stage are successfully resolved, the search for identity continues with less anxiety and more autonomy.

The positive result of this is that children discover they have a *will* and enjoy their new physical and verbal skills. The virtue "will" is not willfulness nor is it willingness, nor even goodwill toward others. It is, says Erikson, "the unbroken determination to exercise free choice as well as self-restraint, in spite of the unavoidable experience of shame and doubt in infancy."

Initiative versus guilt is the next creative challenge when growing up. During the period of ages three to six, the interest begins to shift from wanting autonomy to issues of sexual identity. "Who am I [as a boy or a girl]?" This is a difficult time for children who are rejected if they were not born the "right" sex to please their parents. They reach out to find appropriate models to copy and experience guilt when their efforts are misunderstood, punished, or ridiculed.

Boys take the initiative to seek their mother's attentions; girls want their fathers to notice them. Parents are often confused by typical remarks such as that of a five-year-old boy—"I'm going to marry Mama when I grow up"—or of a five-year-old girl—"I wish Mama would go away so I could have Daddy to myself."

Guilt is not the same as shame. Shame is more likely to stem from a sense of inferiority; guilt is experienced by many people when they fail at their own goals, transgress a rule, or violate a taboo. Shame is self-doubt, deeper than guilt. Shame is a response to the "Don't be" injunctions, whereas guilt is tied in with "Don't be you" injunctions, or "Don't grow up," "Don't be important," "Don't succeed," and the more general injunction of "Don't . . ." ("Don't do this," "Don't do that," "Don't do the other thing," "Just don't.")

The sense of guilt is a common response by children who are overprotected, continually told what's right and wrong, and not encouraged to explore and figure things out for themselves—merely to mind. They break the rules and feel guilty. They may also feel guilty if their parents are emotionally unstable or are overly organized yet emotionally indifferent: "If I could do things perfectly then they would love me."

In each case children tend to feel it is somehow their fault—that they can't do everything perfectly, that they can't really please their parents regardless of how hard they try, or they have the magical belief, "If I had minded, it wouldn't have happened."

In the first two developmental stages, children find out that they are people. In this stage, if the conflict is resolved, they decide what kind of person to be. They develop *purpose* and the capacity to decide on goals. With toys children play out their fantasies and identify with grown-ups—real ones and fantasized ones, as in *Star Wars*. Conscience, often because of internalized parent traditions, begins to develop. Life is seen as having purpose, and the task is to define purpose and goals.

If this developmental crisis is not resolved, goals are not easily established. In later life it may seem easier to "drift with the tide" or leave things to "fate" than to carve out one's own destiny.

Mastery versus inferiority is the next stage of personal development. Mastery refers to being able to meet *academic* challenges in school and *social* challenges in learning how to get along with others. All-boy gangs and all-girl gangs are typical of this period. There is more freedom from home control with more hours spent outside of the home and more chance ɔ begin to master a larger part of the world. Children are very ready for active learning during these years. They are encouraged to be industrious at school and to "get to work." They often do.

Children who are not successful in their efforts to achieve both academic and social success will experience a painful sense of inferiority. Some children may withdraw from interaction with peers and become bookworms or TV addicts. Some begin to act in aggressive or delinquent ways. In many cases the sense of inferiority leads to a decision to be a loner. Later in life such a person may have few or no friends, may work at something that calls for being alone, and may continue to feel inferior to others.

On the positive side, when children are successful socially and successful academically, or proficient in sports or hobbies of some kind, the strength that emerges is the sense of *competence:* "I can do it if I set my mind to it and get to work." A sense of joy comes with the awareness of being able to master a part of the world, to be creative with objects and people.

Identity versus identity diffusion is the crisis of adolescence, roughly between the ages of twelve and eighteen. Puberty with the accompanying glandular changes is a new experience. To find identity—"I am who I am"—is the task. It is also a time when young people question traditional values and ask ideological questions about the meaning of life. One of the major reasons this period is so difficult, especially in the Western world, is that adolescents are kept dependent—by law, society, and parents—for an extended period of time.

Identity diffusion, "I don't know who I am," is the continuing problem when this task is not completed. Drug abuse is one sign that a healthy personal identity has not been achieved. Unwillingness to take responsibility for one's own life is another. This shows in many adolescents who refuse to look for work, or refuse to clean up their own kitchen messes, or organize their homework or free time. "Let Mom do it" is the attitude. Blaming others is a third way because it implies that the blamer is outside the situation and not responsible for what goes wrong.

When identity is established at this age—"I know who I am"—the crisis is resolved. The capacity for *fidelity* is the result. Fidelity is the ability to remain loyal in spite of value contradictions, and identity is the necessary foundation. If this identity crisis is not resolved, loyalty is seen as unimportant. Personal pleasure is the major goal.

It is only after identity is firmly established that the capacity to move into a mutual love relationship becomes possible. Joining clubs, getting married, developing close friends, are all efforts to do this. Without true intimacy a painful sense of loneliness is experienced.

Intimacy versus isolation is the critical issue between ages eighteen and thirty. This is a period when all the unresolved problems around trust or nontrust begin to surface again. The unspoken questions are based on the primary question: "Dare I trust someone enough to be truly intimate, or shall I withdraw, isolate, and insulate myself instead?" "Am I important enough so that someone will come if I need them? Will they accept me as I am with all my unresolved needs? If I love them, will they leave?"

The capacity to *love* with a mutual devotion that quiets antagonisms is the result of this earlier trust issues being solved at last. Strongly based on the awareness of personal identity and decision in fidelity, love of these years is selective, often experienced as a shared identity. Without it, life seems empty and hopeless, and loneliness seems inevitable.

Generativity versus stagnation becomes the issue between the ages of thirty and sixty when the critical decision is whether to give paternal or maternal attention toward others of a younger generation. The successful resolution to this is the development of the virtue of *care*.

Care is an ever-widening "concern for what has been generated by love, necessity, or accident." It is not caring for others out of a sense of duty as some parents do but out of the need to be needed and the need to leave the world a better place. It is caring from a position of free autonomy and is part of self-actualization.

People who are not willing to care for the younger generation often find themselves not needed. They become stagnant, even more disinterested in others, and locked into self-absorption.

Integrity versus despair and disgust about oneself and one's life is the creative challenge that faces people from age sixty on. People who achieve integrity have, before this time, developed acceptance of their parents without wishing the parents had been different. They have also accepted their own life-styles as personal responsibilities out of a sense of personal integrity.

The strength that develops as this crisis is solved is *wisdom*. Without wisdom, there is despair and once more hopelessness. And with wisdom comes a somewhat detached view of life in the face of sure death. The final creative challenge is meeting death with a sense of breaking through with a new kind of freedom.

Caring is a Life-Long Challenge

Liaison

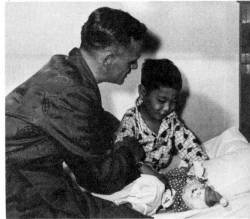

National Archives

"Hey, this is great!"

"I'm going to help you all I can."

"It's a good life even as
it gets shorter."

"Isn't he wonderful!"

Hebble

James

Becoming creative at any and every age involves the use of positive virtues. For example, it is only with *purpose* and *competence* that a person can design a building; it is with *will* that the building is built. Without will, the building would not be built. It is *hope* that sustains the entire creative process.

Becoming an Artist

Often learning how to take care of oneself, to be a good parent to oneself, is like learning how to be an artist. It is affirming the actuality that has already occurred—the being and the doing. It is affirming the potentiality of that which is latent and needs expression. It is learning how to say "yes" to creation, as well as to the self.

Creativity is often associated with becoming an artist. There are many arts. Painting, sculpture, architecture, and writing are but a few. The most important art, however, is this art of living.

Living is a constant challenge. The materials for creating a life that is aesthetically pleasing are always available, yet they are often hard to see. Unfortunately many cultures and parents train people not to see. They train them to adapt to the cliché, "Be happy for what you've got. Think of all the starving . . ."

That's true. When you compare yourself with those less fortunate, you may feel guilty for wanting more and consequently hold back your creative drives. Keep in mind that a pervading sense of guilt is often tied in with the inability to please others, which is the problem when children between the ages of three and six begin to show initiative that is not pleasing to their parents. When this childhood crisis is not solved, purposeful goal setting is difficult.

Amateurs versus Artists

Becoming an artist requires an encouraging inner parent who says, "You can do it." As Ralph Waldo Emerson wrote, "Every artist was once an amateur." Amateurs often enjoy themselves, but seldom do they achieve their highest potentials.

Creative art involves bringing something new into existence—in this case, a new parent who will be your guide, your ally, your friend. The practice of any art requires wishing and wanting, intuiting and creating. It involves studying how to bring something new into existence—a new self. According to Erikson this study involves four factors: discipline, concentration, patience, and ultimate concern.

Amateurs tend to "do their thing" only when they are in the mood, only when they feel like doing it. Artists often are not in the mood for their art. Yet because they are faithful to themselves and to their goals, they use the power of the will for self-discipline. The amateur may say:

"I'll do it when I have time" or

"I'll do it when I'm in the mood" or

"I'll do it some other day."

The disciplined artist will affirm something like:

"I'll start the project tomorrow at nine."

"I'm going to focus my energies now."

"I'm tired, but I'll do it anyway."

Amateurs also tend to "do their thing" spasmodically. They are unwilling to concentrate, are distracted easily, and have a low level of persistence. They may leave their creation often to do things such as answering the phone or getting a cup of coffee. Whereas a temporary break in intensity often allows new creative ideas to emerge from the unconscious, a casual concentration dissipates energy. Thus the amateur may say:

"I want to be spontaneous and not concentrate."

"I just can't concentrate on anything."

"I don't want to concentrate today."

In contrast, the artist who is willing to put energy into concentrating may say:

"I do not want to be interrupted for three hours."

"I am not going to answer the phone or door."

"I'm going to focus my attention on this problem."

Creating art is also negated by people who are impatient to get it right the first time. These are people who drive themselves as though they were slave drivers. The inner Child may try harder and harder, yet it never satisfies the impatient inner Parent. When this is the case, a person may stop being cre-

Creativity Takes Many Forms

Hebble

National Archives

"Let's build a castle
or dig a hole."

"Let's make up our
own game."

"What do you think of it?"

"I like the way I
designed the program."

Stock, Boston, Inc.

Hebble

ative because of not feeling fast enough or good enough. The impatient amateur might say:

"It doesn't have to be perfect if it's just done."

"Oh, I'll never get it done so why try."

"I'll hurry just to prove I'm not lazy."

The artist who is willing to persist patiently might affirm:

"I want excellence even if it takes more time."

"I may be slow but I like the results."

"I don't have to hurry just to get finished."

Ultimate concern involves priorities, and to be an artist at living needs to have a high priority if it is to be achieved. Ultimate concern shows in people who are disciplined, who are able to concentrate, and who are patient with themselves in the learning process. Amateurs without ultimate concerns might say:

"It doesn't matter; there's always tomorrow."

"Other things are more important."

"Who cares! Not me!"

People who are artists at living set high priorities, which shows in their actions and words:

"The quality of life is what is important to me."

"Designing my new life is crucial to me."

"Discovering what it means to break free is my priority."

Notes from a Workshop

Jean was a daydreamer and procrastinator until she learned how to be a good parent to herself.

"I used to daydream a lot about what I might do someday if my ship came in. The ideas and images would just float in and out of my head. Then one day when the youngest started school, I became aware that the new parent in my head was suddenly encouraging me to go to school. Also suddenly I wanted to develop myself in new ways.

"It was scary. I didn't know how. I didn't know if any college would take me at my age and my lousy high school grades. I was scared stiff, and in spite of that scare I *decided*, 'I will do it and I will do it now.'

"So I created a plan. Instead of just applying to one school, I applied to several so I would have more information and options. Finally, I found one that gave me some academic units for my life skills as wife, mother, and community volunteer. The school was flexible, it saved me time, and now I'm back to imagining what the next step after graduation might be. I almost feel like 'the world's my oyster,' and I know I'm more creative than I ever dreamed was possible, not at painting but at living. I give myself a lot of compliments these days because I'm at last being a firm parent to me."

Breakthrough VII—Breaking Through with Creativity

If you've read this far, you've probably become aware of several patterns in your life and discovered how they developed. You also may have discovered that you have been stuck at a particular developmental age because you did not have the kind of parenting you needed to solve the crisis or creative challenge.

The purpose of this breakthrough is to use your creative thinking for possible solutions without judgment or analyzing whether they would work. That comes later.

Creative writing: Lots of people claim they can't write, that they are not creative. They are usually wrong. If you don't believe me, experiment for yourself.

Select any problem area that gives you trouble and write a four-minute story. Start with "Once upon a time there was a _____
_____." Write as fast as you can. Do not stop to think. Write no longer than four minutes. The limited time will help you be creative. Now write.

After you have finished, evaluate the position you took. How does it reflect the new ways you are learning of how to be a good parent to yourself? In what way was it creative?

Problem area quiz Following is a list of the symptoms. This is a quiz so you can see what you've learned. Look at the problems and fill in the blanks. What do they indicate is wrong and unresolved?

Lack of hope indicates _____.

Lack of purpose indicates _____.

Lack of competence indicates _____.

Lack of fidelity indicates _____.

Lack of love indicates _____.

Lack of caring indicates _____.

Lack of wisdom indicates _____.

It's OK to go back and look at the diagram on page 151. Do you get some new clues for your reparenting?

Strengths you developed   Let your memories float back in time to the various periods in your life when you felt a sense of power and strength and when you felt powerless. Continue the process for each age level.

Ages when I felt strong	*The strength I felt was*	*What I did with my strength*

Ages when I felt weak	*The weakness was due to lack of*	*What I did with my weakness*

Strengths you need Evaluate the strengths or virtues you have now and the ones you might be missing. Then fill in the blanks in the following sentences.

The kind of a parent who could have helped me develop the virtue of _____ is one who would _____ and _____ and _____.

I need that kind of new parent. Therefore I will act in the following parenting ways to myself _____

_____

_____ until I frequently experience that inner strength that comes with the virtue of _____.

Now record in your journal how you are creating new strengths with self-reparenting.

Contracting For Freedom

8

Many are stubborn in pursuit of the path they have chosen, few in pursuit of the goal.

  Nietzsche

To "contract" for freedom is to choose a goal, to be flexible in taking differ- ent paths to reach this goal, and, at the same time, to remain stubbornly faithful to the goal itself.

The capacity for fidelity is an achievement of adolescence if young people solve the dilemma of knowing who they are (identity) versus not knowing who they are (identity confusion). Fidelity is the ability to remain loyal "in spite of . . ." Being faithful is not always easy. It requires the use and posi- tive strength of the will.

Of course some people's personal growth is interfered with. They may not have developed their potential strengths for trusting or willing or having a sense of purpose or feeling competent socially and academically in child- hood. Yet trust, will, purpose, and competence *can* be developed in later life. A new parent who encourages the development of these strengths pro- vides strong incentives for the capacity to think clearly, to think creatively, and to remain faithful to chosen goals.

This chapter will show you how you can use your will and your capacity to be faithful to yourself and to reach your freedom goals. You will learn new techniques for deciding how to set goals and for deciding how to reach them.

You will discover how the "old you" can sabotage or undermine your goals and how your new Parent can be your permanent friend and protector, fighting against negative influences that interfere with your freedom.

To do this, the thinking, rational Adult part of you will learn to act as a substitute parent. It will *team up* with your new parent. This will increase your power to get what you want and need and increase your freedom to express your potentials.

Fidelity to Change

Fidelity, as it is being used in this chapter, does not refer exclusively to being loyal to others, which is being able to enter into a mutually loving relationship. It is used here to refer to being loyal to yourself. Fidelity and loyalty can be used interchangeably. The etymology of the word *loyalty* reflects the French root *loi,* or "law." Laws are built on contracts.

Contracts are agreements. In learning how to be a good parent to yourself, they are agreements to change and update the old parent you have in your head to a new parent who asks you to make a decision in favor of freedom.

When people make decisions to be faithful to themselves, their contracting can become a reality. Breaking through to freedom is not breaking out of a situation solely from an attitude of defiance and rebellion; it requires careful planning to be effective. To escape is to be free *from* something. This is a necessary step but not the same as being free *to* experience the fullness of living.

To live fully includes the risk of failing. This risk can be minimized with a sense of determination and the use of the will.

Determination and Will

Wanting is to begin to reach out and to form rudimentary plans. It is more than dreaming. It is the experience of natural power: "I want what I want and I want it now." Deciding to get what is wanted is possible because of will. *Will is determination to act in spite of self-doubt.* It is the developmental task of children between the ages of one and a half and three and leads to a youthful belief in the freedom to choose because of experiencing some measure of autonomy.

The Need for Change

National Archives

"What must I do for freedom?"

Stock, Boston, Inc.

"I wonder if I can survive."

"It's time for a change."

FEMINISM LIVES

Herwig/Stock, Boston, Inc.

Will is decision making and organizing one's energy toward a specified goal. "I will do it, no matter what" are words that point to self-assurance in spite of self-doubt. When people use their will, they experience the power that comes with making decisions. People who continually procrastinate often express their lack of will. "I just can't decide" or "I'm too tired to decide" are frequent complaints of procrastinators. Such people may wish for something, yet they don't use the energy to get it. If they did, they would use their wills and discover the power of the will.

Organizing oneself requires purpose, deliberation, and the use of the will. The value of organizing oneself is that it allows people to do something about which they may feel ambivalent or may not want to do—such as studying for an important examination when physically tired or doing necessary exercises in this book as part of learning self-reparenting.

Children who are overorganized by their parents and not allowed autonomy may not learn how to recognize and use their wills. Later in life when their very existence is threatened, as in an earthquake or fire or when seriously ill or hurt, they may not know how to call on this inner power. Their will is weak rather than strong. Either passively or anxiously they may wait for "destiny" or "fate" or for some real or imagined "authority" to direct their lives."

It is not unusual for people entering their middle years to turn helplessly to parents or parent substitutes for advice and nurturing. More than a few revert to early adolescent behavior. Whereas in some cases it is satisfying to follow advice without evaluating, it may be a reflection of an untrained will. People often choose to regress to earlier stages of development to avoid responsibility.

The failure of the will to develop is an important problem. Frequently the lament is heard, "I can't do it." This lament may be real or imagined. The external signs of those who have given up on wishing and willing are apathy and passivity. The cost is great.

It's all too evident that *wishing* only sometimes leads to action and satisfaction. *Willing* usually leads to action, but satisfaction may not be the result. The use of power is necessary. Will without power is merely wish. Wish without will is merely a daydream. Wishing can lead to decisions that involve action and require will. Willingness to act is to have the power to change.

In the current search for freedom, the widespread encouragement to "know yourself" so you can change what you want to change wouldn't make sense without the possibility of choice and the capacity to use wish and will for growth rather than for repression.

People experience the will, according to Roberto Assagioli, as "intelligent energy, directed toward a definite aim, having a purpose. . . . It is a unifying force." He believes the will can be trained and needs to be. The training is in three phases: first, the recognition that the will exists; second, the realization of having a will; and third, the discovery of being a will.

In any case, experiencing needs and wishes, wants and will, is part of the human search for freedom. Wishing and wanting stem from drives and needs. They precede willing. Yet wishing is not just associated with infantile needs, as some maintain. To be in touch with a wish is to be in touch with hope and determination and the desire to change the future in creative ways.

Your Developing Will

Recall your childhood and some of the daydreams you had for your future.

Did these daydreams materialize?

If so, what was the process?

How was your will involved?

If they did not materialize, was it because you felt unable to mobilize your will?

How would the ideal parent you are creating for yourself encourage your use of your will?

The Developing Will

"And I _will_ hit that ball."

"Hurray! A home run!"

"I will catch it. I know I will."

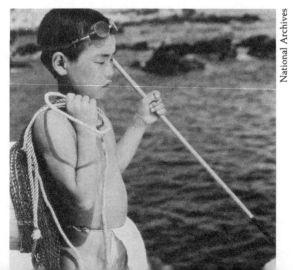

The Will-to-Power

The power of the will is not the same as the will-to-power. The power of the will is based on using personal strength to take charge of one's own life.

The will-*to*-power is based on efforts to take charge of someone else's life. It is a deviation from the basic human striving for doing well and for actualization of potentials. Alfred Adler, one of the "greats" in the field of psychology, noted that there are three possible causes for this personality problem of the will-to-power. First are the physical organic weaknesses (inferiorities) that may occur before birth during the process of fetal development or as the result of illness, infection, or accident; second are the educational errors by parents and teachers who demand too much or who use ridicule or lies such as, "You dumb and ugly kid," to control children. Third are the social causes that come from marginal economic and social conditions within a family or community.

Later in life the will-to-power shows in a person who seeks superiority by trying to be better than anyone else—in a class, on a job, and so forth. This person may feel jealousy and hatred and show high ambition, arrogance, "one-upmanship," or self-righteousness, acting with an "I'm right, you're wrong" orientation.

The opposite of the person with the will-to-power is the person who tries to control others by helplessness. This person may feel anxious and inadequate and act shy and weak, use poor judgment, and get others to make decisions. By acting helpless, this person also uses the will-to-power—trying to control others into caretaking roles.

Your Childhood Will-to-Power

Perhaps you are aware of a development of your will-to-power, perhaps not. The things that lead to this personality problem are physical organic inferiorities, poor teaching, or economic or cultural impoverishment.

Think back to your school years. Was there anything about your body that you believed was inferior?

Was there anything about your school that was too hard? Were you teased or punished in school? Taught erroneous ideas?

What about your family and the way you lived? Were you impoverished in some way so that you felt trapped instead of free?

If you answered "Yes" to any of these questions, how did you use your will-to-power then? What about it now?

What kind of ideal parent messages do you need for yourself to reduce the sense of inadequacy or one-upmanship?

Notes From a Workshop

A thirty-five-year-old woman who came in for counseling had many signs of anger. Her face looked pinched, her jaw and fists often clenched, her body was tight, and her voice and words were bitter. When asked about her anger, she aggressively stated that she felt as if she had been angry since birth. When asked how long she was going to hang on to her anger, she claimed even more aggressively, "Until the day I die." My only comment on this was, "What a waste of a lifetime."

During the process of therapy she worked on several difficult interpersonal problems and began to resolve them except for her lifelong resentment of her mother. It was not until she started to evaluate her friendships with other women that she saw the connection. "Ye gods," she shouted, "I don't have any women friends I can trust and if I did, I'd probably push them away just like my mother did with me."

The cost of *not* changing had been high for this woman, both physically and emotionally, and her life had been without hope. The cost of changing would involve some painful feelings. It would require time, energy, and commitment.

A few weeks later, when she had thought about the poor parenting her own mother had had as a little girl, she made several important decisions. First, that she didn't need to act toward others as her mother had acted toward her. Second, that she could forgive her mother and seek to understand her. Third, that she could learn how to be caring and nurturing instead of angry and hostile. Fourth, that she would stop wasting any more of her life and instead use it productively for her own freedom.

The delivery date she gave herself for a new parent was six months. She fulfilled her contract to the day and was free at last from her own bitterness.

Choosing to Change

Throughout your life you have made many changes. Some of them may have been forced on you by other people or circumstances. Some you have freely chosen.

Is there a pattern in your choosing to change? How do you evaluate the cost? How do you evaluate the payment schedule? How do you evaluate the product and the delivery date for that product?

Introduction to Contracting

A contract is an agreement based on a decision. For example, people who decide to buy a car or house or piece of furniture usually sign some kind of contract specifying the cost, the payment schedule, and the delivery date, and so forth. The same elements are present when contracting to develop a new parent in the Parent ego state who will function in positive ways to your inner Child. Your initial cost has been the purchase of this book. Your payment schedule has been the time and energy you have invested in this project. Now the delivery date is up to you. You can speed it up or delay it indefinitely.

Choosing to change involves making firm decisions to take charge of one's life and live it more abundantly. There are six very basic questions to use when establishing a contract. These become a plan for change. They can be elaborated upon or expanded, or subsidiary contracts can be made on the basis of the original contract. As you think about these questions, consider the needs and wants of your inner Child and the traditions and attitudes of your old Parent. Take into consideration the updating you have done in creating a new Parent for yourself.

If you have studied the process in this book of how to be a good parent to yourself, you have already changed some important aspects in your personality and in your life. You are able to see yourself more clearly; you are able to hear yourself and your inner dialogue with more understanding; you are able to be more in touch with your emotions and more aware of your senses. You have been, and continue to be, breaking through to new freedom. And it feels good because you are becoming, more and more, a good parent to yourself.

The six following questions are the foundations for all effective contracting. They are:

> What do I want that would enhance my life?
> What do I need to do to get what I want?
> What am I willing to do?
> How would I measure my success?
> How might I sabotage myself?
> If I do, what positive step can I then take?

The Process of Contracting

Breaking through to freedom is a lifelong task, never fully achieved. New goals always emerge as though on the horizon, yet the process itself of moving toward the horizon of freedom is exciting and valuable. The process lends meaning to life and helps answer the questions, "Who am I?" and "What am I doing?"

What do I want that would enhance my life? The word *enhance* is an important word in this first contracting step. Many desires that people have do not enhance life; they discolor it, dilute it, or in time, destroy it. To enhance is to make something more desirable, to increase its beauty and value. Therefore, an enhanced life is a life with high vitality, freedom, power, and trust.

What do I need to do to get what I want? The emphasis in this question is on what *I* need to do, not on what others could do to make me happy. What *I* need to do may involve risk, cost, and courage. I may feel as if it's too big a risk or too costly to undertake or as if I'm not courageous enough to make the effort. If so, it's time to ask the next question.

What am I willing to do? Many people know what they *need* to do, but they are *not willing* to do it. "What am I willing to do?" requires a careful assessment of time, energy, motivation, and, again, cost. Changing a life by making contracts that enhance it will cost something. The cost may be an interpersonal relation, a sum of money, a safe situation, emotional security, a block of time, and so forth.

The cost, say, of losing a job because of speaking up to the boss may be more than the Child can tolerate without "kicking up a fuss" or getting sick. If so, back off and choose a different goal. If the inner Child is too unhappy with the change, the contract won't work. The cost may also be too much for the Parent. If so, back off and modify it until it's endurable. The Adult may also go out of gear if the contract is beyond its capacity. The Adult may need more information and education to function smoothly and mediate between the opinions and traditions of the Parent and the feelings and adaptations of the Child.

The *will* is at stake. Willing is not the same as wishing. Willing is decision based on solving the crisis of autonomy versus self-doubt of one-and-a-half to three-year-olds. This resolution is necessary because *if I doubt myself I may not be* willing to take a risk, and my emerging new parent may need to encourage me to do so. If I get through this crisis and have some measure of inner freedom and autonomy, then I am willing to opt for things that will enhance my life.

Naturally if I opt for something that will interfere and destroy other people's lives, mine will not really be enhanced. Sooner or later another person's unhappiness is likely to affect me. In that situation I will not be successful in the art of living. To succeed at the expense of someone else is to fail in the deepest sense.

How would I measure my success? In the world of today, success is usually measured in terms of achieving power, prestige, or possessions. Whereas some of that is fine, to measure success as the art of living requires breaking free from the "standard" evaluations of a "standard society."

Therefore I can measure my success only if I am faithful to my goals and to the process I take for reaching them, which includes loving myself and being loved by others.

If my goal is to lose weight, or get a new job, or take a two-week vacation, I can measure my success. If it is to find inner peace, perhaps my lowered blood pressure will show it; if it is to recover vitality, perhaps I can assess my progress by an inner buoyancy of confidence and joy. Each of these successes will be aided by my new and friendly parent whom I have designed for myself.

If I make contracts that are impractical or cannot be measured, such as "cutting down on smoking," I need to sharpen them. If I make one of smoking only three cigarettes a day instead of two packs, that's measurable. Therefore with each contract I make, I must find specific ways to measure my self-love, my fidelity, and the use of my will to keep my promises.

How might I sabotage myself? To sabotage myself is to undermine my own goals. It is to give in to that part of me that may not want to succeed because it feels dumb and ugly. If I sabotage myself, I justify, rationalize, and make excuses. I "cop out" and say "I can't" instead of saying "I will—no matter what."

If I discover that the goal I *thought* I wanted is not what I really want, what then? Well, I might sabotage myself, giving up and proclaiming, "I've failed again so why try?" instead of changing my contract so that I can make it.

Sometimes I may be just too tired, or too depressed, or too anxious to work on keeping my commitments, so again I might give in. What do I need to do instead?

What's my next positive step? If I do sabotage myself, what can I do about it instead of sitting around feeling bad or denying it by frantic activity? Well, I can cancel that contract and make a new one that is more in line with what I actually need and want and am able to achieve. I can set smaller goals, reach them, and build on my successes until I have more freedom to tackle the big things in life.

For example, my contract might be to become a gourmet cook in one month, yet the budget may not allow for many new expenditures. Therefore my contract might need to be modified to learn how to cook one gourmet meal or one special dish a month.

As another example, I might have a contract to develop closeness with a particular person. That person may not have the same desire or may not have the time to put into the relationship. Therefore my contract needs to be changed so that potential success is a real possibility. My sense of freedom will increase if I have flexible goals and various paths to travel when seeking the goals.

Notes from a Workshop

"What I want," said Jane, "is to lose thirty pounds of weight. I'm tired of looking ugly, and it's dumb of me to stay the way I am. I want to change.

"What I need to do is to clear out the cupboards and refrigerator of all tempting food that I eat when I'm feeling depressed or lonesome. I also need to exercise by walking eight blocks to the bus from my house and not take my car. I also need to walk from store to store when I go to the shopping mall, usually once a week, instead of dragging myself in and out of my car to drive only fifty yards or so.

"My problem is that I've made many such promises before and haven't kept them. I'm not faithful to myself, although I am to other people. That's interesting to think about; evidently I am able to be faithful so I guess I just need to *decide* to be that way to me.

"OK, but I'm not willing to get rid of all the food. It would be like 'quitting cold turkey' and I don't think it would work. However, *I am willing to throw away all the ice cream and other goodies* in the freezer, even if it costs me money, or give that food to one of my skinny friends. And I *won't* buy any more sweet stuff. Also, although I won't walk in the rain, *I am willing to walk.* I'll do it in good weather, and I'll use the stairs instead of the elevator at work.

"I'll measure my success on the scales. And I'll weigh myself each morning the very first thing. I know that my success may not show immediately, yet it will certainly show in two weeks' time. In one month I'll lose at least six pounds of my goal of thirty pounds.

"I might sabotage myself if I talk to myself with a critical, sarcastic parent voice or an overindulgent voice, or if I set goals that are too difficult to reach, or if I procrastinate on getting rid of the ice cream.

The Need to Decide

Kafman

Riddle

"Will I or won't I?"

"What do I want?"

"How long?"

"Shall we always
go on like this?"

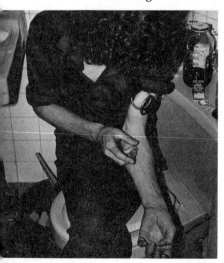

Stock, Boston, Inc.

James

"If I do sabotage myself, the positive step I will take is to be gentle and firm with myself. I will evaluate my contract and decide if it has to be modified. I will remind myself that I'm learning to be faithful to me and using my will in new ways. Instead of overindulging myself by giving in to feelings of guilt or anger, I'll pick myself up and continue toward my goal."

Other Contract Considerations

Many contracts fail because people deny or forget their strengths and other personal resources that they can use to reach their goals. Business people call upon their personal and corporate resources to carry out a contract effectively. In fact, contract deadlines and stipulations usually demand the full and efficient use of resources. Similarly, in contracting to be a good parent to oneself, the more skills, talents, abilities, and native gifts people can call upon, the better.

Another important consideration is the influence of friends, colleagues, and family when they hear about contracts for change. Sometimes it is useful for others to know; sometimes it is not and may become a sabotage. Even in business, some contracts need to be kept secret, for their success depends on an element of surprise. On the other hand, the success of some contracts may be enhanced when they are made public. In contracting, the person making the contract needs to consider whom to tell and when it would be helpful to tell.

Contract revisions are sometimes necessary if a contract is not clear, or is too difficult to achieve, or loses its meaning. Good business people are aware of their limits. They know that a contract too big for them may do more harm than good to their company. They also wisely design contracts that are not too rigid and allow room for bargaining and revision. They know that situations change, and such factors often necessitate changing contracts. For example, a person who contracts for an expensive travel vacation may need to revise the plans if costs escalate or income is reduced.

The Price of Caring

Disappointment is sometimes experienced when contracts need changing. One of the most important antidotes for disappointment is self-care and care from others. Disappointment sometimes feels like a poison, filling a person's being until that person may feel "sick unto death." If you're that person, you really need to learn how to take loving, nurturing parental care of yourself.

Care is often an effective cure. It brings hope to the rejected and down-trodden, forgiveness to those who feel failure and guilt, comfort to the sick and lonely, and healing even to those who injure themselves with feelings of hatred and vengeance. Some people are aware of their own negative feelings and wish that, somehow or another, they would be freed of them. Some people are aware that others are also enslaved and want to help them—if only they knew how.

Although it has been said, "greater love has no man than this, then that he lay down his life for a friend," not everyone is called on to risk their lives in the caring of others, everyone is called upon from the deepest center of their being to break free. Breaking free includes allowing oneself to care deeply for others and encourage others to care also.

Caring is a risk, yet people take risks because they care about the possible outcome and hope the outcome will be satisfying. Caring also carries a price. Caring involves weighing values, often clarifying what the values are. For example, if you take time to take care of yourself physically and emotionally, you may not have as much time to take care of others. This might cost you a friendship.

If you care about your own career and put your primary time and energy into it, this devotion may cost you your marriage or your children's love. Or the price may be the time you need for exercising or the time you want for developing a hobby.

The reverse is also true. If you put a lot of time and energy into caring for others, you may not have much left for yourself.

Caring is precarious. Deciding on what kind of loving care to give yourself is difficult. Deciding on what kind of loving care to give others is also difficult.

When people contract to *give* care to themselves and others as intelligent, loving parents would do, they do not do it impulsively, without thinking. They weigh the costs of caring and the costs of not caring. Caring shows in actions, not just in words.

On the other hand, when people contract to *accept* care, they can also weigh the costs. They may find it easier to give to receive, to respond to other people's needs than to ask for care for themselves. They may believe that asking for help is a sign they are weak or incompetent. I don't believe that. Although independence is fine, persons who are free can recognize and accept their own need for care and develop the strength to care for others.

The Price of Love and Care

Think about one of the goals you have designed for your new parent so that you will experience more freedom. Then evaluate the cost:

One of my goals is _____.

What I might gain from it is _____.

What it might cost me is _____.

Is the cost too great or the path to the goal too threatening for me at this time?

If it is, how can I show more caring to myself?

Owning the Freedom to Change

To own something is to be able to say, "This is mine; it belongs to me." Many people willingly give away what belongs to them . . . their time, their energy, their possessions. They do this out of love or compassion. Others may reluctantly give away what belongs to them . . . their time, their energy, their possessions. They do this out of a sense of duty. Some give to manipulate others. Some give from a position of fear or guilt, believing that they don't "deserve" to have anything or to be their "own person." And many, throughout the world, do not have what belongs to them; their bodies, their self-esteem, their opportunities for life and liberty and the pursuit of happiness are wrenched away by those who are power mad.

You may have given up your power to change for any or several of these reasons. Now is the time to reclaim it, to own your power, to say "Yes" to yourself. You need your love. You need to say "No" to you and to other people who demean, ridicule, prevent, or punish you for "owning your power."

Self-reparenting includes learning how and when to say "Yes" and how and when to say "No" to yourself.

"The No's Have It." People who have had overindulgent or indifferent parents need to be a good parent to themselves by setting reasonable limits for the inner Child. "No, you can't mistreat your body as you do." "No, you can't fog up your mind with drugs and propaganda and crazy leftover ideas from childhood that interfere with your growth." "No, you can't hold back and repress the inner core of you that seeks meaning and ultimate concern and the spiritual dimension of living."

As you become a good parent to you, you may need to say to yourself, "Stop doing that. It's not healthy." "Stop the self-indulgence." "Stop complaining." "Stop trying to be perfect." "Stop looking for success through other people's eyes." "Stop disowning your own power."

"All in Favor Say Aye." When using a "No" or "Stop" with yourself, it is often helpful to replace it with a "Yes" and adding the word *instead.* "Instead" emphasizes the choices you have.

"Yes, you can take time to care for your body *instead* of using your time mostly for others." "Yes, you can study or learn something new in other ways *instead* of staying confused and feeling intellectually inferior." "Yes, you can meditate on the meaning of life and experience the spirit within *instead* of denying the possibility that this is a source of power."

Beverly explained the Yes-No process: "I used to always say 'No' to myself; then I learned to say 'Yes.' It was a very different experience. I used to say 'No' so often! It was like I was telling myself, 'No, you can't do that' or 'No, you mustn't feel that,' even 'No, it's bad to think that' and 'No, it's crazy to believe that.'

"Now that I've learned to say 'Yes' to myself with my new Parent, it's so different. I don't just say 'Yes' to what I want to *do* or 'Yes' to what I *feel,* or *think,* or *believe.* It's 'Yes' to *me.*

"Now I know 'I am who I am.' Just that, no details! My 'Yes' to me reinforces my freedom my new Parent gives me. Now that I know I am who I am, I've got the power to be Me, Myself, and I."

Breakthrough VIII—Setting Contracts

Self-reparenting involves Adult decisions. Decisions lead to contracts made by your Adult who (1) will accept parenting responsibility, (2) will not act like an irresponsible parent, and (3) will be committed to staying with your Child until the task is finished.

The "Ayes" and "Nays"   Make a list of the ways you currently say "No" and "Yes" to yourself.

Study the list and consider, Do you need your new ideal parent to say "No" or "Yes" to you in different ways?

How I say "yes" to myself	*Changes I need to make*
_____	_____
_____	_____
_____	_____

How I say "no" to myself	*Changes I need to make*
_____	_____
_____	_____
_____	_____

Evaluating Contracts   Effective contracts need to be reasonable and measurable. List some that would enhance your life.

My Wants and Needs	Contracts I Need	How I Would Measure Success

Ego States and Self-Sabotaging   Many people sabotage their own contracts so they do not get what they want and need. Check out the sabotaging potentials of each of your ego states:

Parent beliefs, that could sabotage my contracts	How I might use these to sabotage myself	How I could avoid this self-sabotage

Information I need for my Adult	How I might ignore information	How I could avoid this self-sabotage

Contracts that seem too hard to my Child	How I might use my timidity and fear	How I could avoid this self-sabotage

Sabotaging by others   Many people, feeling helpless or confused, allow others to sabotage them. Become aware of who has this power that could be used against you, what they would do, and how you could respond.

Who might interfere with my contracts	What might they do (be specific)	How might I join them in sabotaging me	What I could do instead

On the basis of your new awareness, do you need to alter your contracts or make additional ones? If so, do this caring act for yourself. Record this in your journal.

From Hope to Joy

9

On with the dance! let joy be unconfined.
   Byron

Joy is lightness, it is laughter, it is release, it is dance. It is the result of old hopes and it stimulates new hopes. Joy often comes as a surprise that lifts the heart and heals the body. It comes from within, especially as you choose ways that enhance life. It comes from without, especially as you are open to the moments and majesty of existence.

This chapter will help you understand the importance of hope in the lifelong commitment to breaking free. You will discover that as your skills in recognizing and dealing with problems of living increase, so will your hope, your pleasure, your satisfactions, your experiences of joy, and your deeper sense of happiness.

Is the Glass Half-Full or Half-Empty?

Most people have either a basically positive or a basically negative attitude toward life. People who look at themselves and their needs from a basically negative perspective say things like, "Well, I *only* have . . . therefore I can't . . . " Like a person who says the glass of water is half-empty, they see the worst. Confront them by reminding them of the positive things in their lives, and they will respond with a comment that reflects, "Yes, but the glass of water *is* half empty." And the complaints will continue.

In contrast, some people see only the positive; therefore they see no need to change. They fantasize that all glasses are full and running over with goodness. Having a Pollyanna attitude, they look at the world through rose-colored glasses or, like some horses, wear blinders so as not to be disturbed by what they might see that would distract them from their chosen path.

In contrast to both of these attitudes, a person who looks more realistically at a difficult problem and does so from a perspective of seeing a glass half-full instead of half-empty is one who has hope and determination for breaking free. Hope is good medicine.

Notes from a Workshop

Marlene and Robert were moving to a new location and life-style. After much deliberation they had decided that "moving up the organizational ladder" was not conducive to their well-being. They complained of feeling half-empty, with less interest in life.

"We're so *drained* by the whole setup—commuting to work for two hours a day each way, then rushing home to do the chores or not rushing home and instead spending too much time and money in bars. We're getting empty fast and already, at age thirty-two, the bottom of our relationship is close to going dry. We don't want that to happen and we're not going to let it. We're going to change our way of living and do it now."

Several members of the workshop tried to persuade Marlene and Robert not to move, not to give up their jobs, not to change their life-style—to no avail. Marlene and Robert recognized their enslavement; they hoped for freedom. It was hope that led them to the decision to do something.

Certainly this couple's choice to build a simple cabin and live off the land would not be the choice everyone would or should make. Some people would say this couple was running away from their problems. Maybe so. However, there is a strong cultural movement of back to simple basics. Many people are discovering that power, possessions, and prestige do not necessarily lead to breaking free. These people are willing to pioneer in new ways and help each other do so in many new forms of community. They no longer trust the old cultural parent who seems so economically oriented at the expense of other values. They have developed a new parent who encourages them to think in new ways, to act with hope.

The Nature of Hope

Hope is so basic to existence that most people agree with Cicero that while there's life, there's hope.

It is the basic ingredient that motivates people to discover ways of breaking free. As people become loving parents to themselves, they become strongly aware of the incredible power of hope.

Hoping is looking to the future with confidence. Hope is not the same as optimism. Optimism implies just *waiting* for things to turn out well without putting effort into making them do so. Hope implies being involved in the process. It leads to decisions to fight for health and freedom against destructive and dehumanizing forces in life.

Hope is the foundation of all other strengths, the basic factor that motivates people to design plans for breaking free. A new encouraging Parent helps the inner Child rediscover hope.

Some people, however, claim that hope is merely "wishful thinking." I think that is wrong. Whereas unrealistic hope may lead to disaster, the lack of hope often leads to despair, even decay.

Without hope, people do not strive or struggle to break free. Their emotional and physical health often begins to give way. Having taken the position, "What's the use? There's nothing left to hope for," they see the world from a negative perspective. Their lack of hope undermines their power to use the will to make decisions and to keep caring commitments.

What is the balance of hope versus hopelessness, and how can the capacity to hope be used to enhance living? Why is it that people, when sick, "hope" for wellness, when lonesome "hope" for love, when guilty "hope" for forgiveness, when afraid "hope" for courage, when enslaved "hope" for freedom? Surely it is because hope is so basic to being itself and so necessary for "doing." In response to the "Who am I?" and "What am I doing?" questions posed in chapter 1, a person might respond, "I am one who hopes" and "What I am doing depends on what I am hoping for."

Free at Last

National Archives

"From concentration to liberation."

"We were born for freedom."

World Wide Photos

HOSTAGES FREE!

Hope is personal and interpersonal. At a personal level, it sustains people in the depths of despair. It also reverses despair and sustains them when they are planning for the future or when transcending immediate pain in the "now."

Your Use of Hope

Recall a problem that you once solved. How did your hope function at a personal or interpersonal level?

Think of a current problem. How is your hope functioning at personal and interpersonal levels?

Focus on one of your dreams for the future. Do you need to release your capacity to hope more fully?

If so, what kind of new, caring parent messages do you need to use with yourself?

Hope as Interpersonal Expectancy

At an interpersonal level, hope is the expectancy of external help. We live by hope, whether we recognize that we do or not. This means that what we do is often based on the belief that it will get us somewhere even if we don't know where or what the somewhere is. Living in hope also means that in the process of getting somewhere, we hope to meet others on the path who will be people of goodwill and willing to help.

Many pessimists do not believe in the concept of help from others that is freely given. They see all interpersonal relations as bartering: "You scratch my back and I'll scratch yours." Or if the backscratching is not even, they assume the back scratcher is saving up feelings of self-righteousness and superiority. This is not my experience. Many people have given freely to me without thought of return. I believe I have done the same because helping others is part of humanity, part of the nature of being.

Asking for help, needing help, is also part of being human. Yet many people learn in childhood that asking and hoping will bring them nothing but rejection. They repress the need for interpersonal help and instead select a compulsive pattern of "being strong" as a life-style. "I can't trust anyone else" becomes their basic belief structure; "therefore I'll do it myself" is their conclusion.

When at some later time in life they discover "doing it myself" doesn't work, hopelessness sets in. Hopelessness is choosing to maintain a basically negative attitude. It is the avoidance of reality. It is the cause of despair.

Disappointment and Hope

Let your memory return to your childhood. Recall several situations in which you experienced deep disappointment because of what you hoped for from someone else.

Then try to recall what you *did* about your disappointment and what you *said* to yourself.

Now consider some recent disappointments in your life. What do you do with your feelings? What do you say to yourself?

Is there a negative pattern from childhood that remains with you now? If so, what self-reparenting do you need to change this pattern?

The Challenge to Forgive

Many things interfere with people's capacities to hope, to trust themselves and others, to make contracts, to enjoy life, to play, think, work, and love. Holding on to resentments is a block to the reestablishment of trust. Trust and hope is restored when forgiving occurs.

Learning to trust, rather than distrust, is the crisis and challenge of infancy. If parents are predictable, caring, and able to meet their infant's needs, the infant begins to develop the capacity to trust others. Hope flourishes. People with this experience feel able to set goals and achieve them.

However, later in life those who do trust may, of course, be betrayed. When this occurs, they first feel surprised, as though a rug had been quickly pulled out from under their feet. Next they feel hurt as though, with the pull of the rug, they have landed flat on their faces. Then, as they seek to pull themselves together, they may experience feelings such as:

confusion because of the unpredictability of the trust breaking;

inadequacy for not recognizing the signs it was coming;

anger because of the hurt.

To retaliate for a broken trust, some people look for ways to strike back. They decide to "get even," as they experience feelings such as:

vengeance because of being hurt;

hatred because of being betrayed;

envy because of being let down.

Other people respond differently to a broken trust. They give up instead of fighting back. Their feelings may be:

fear because of the pain;

indifference because of no caring;

despair because of no hope.

It seems as though when people get close and begin to trust each other, they also feel vulnerable because of their potential for being hurt and misunderstood. This vulnerability is sometimes based on reality; often it is a replay of childhood experiences.

Because hurting is so painful, and perhaps inevitable, learning how to forgive oneself and others is a requirement. To forgive means *to grant pardon without holding resentment.*

Many people say things such as, "I forgive you *but* . . . " This reveals an attitude that is basically *non*forgiving. The implication of the word *but* is "I won't really forget the pain, and I'm likely to hold on to my resentment about it."Setting contracts to forgive is a challenge. Meeting the challenge leads to new freedom. Try it!

Forgiving Your Parents, Forgiving Yourself

Start first with considering whether you are willing to forgive your parents or substitute parents. Fill in the blanks in the following sentence:

"If I forgave you [Mom, Dad, Grandma, brother, sister, etc.] for [whatever happened], I would be able to trust you because _____.

_____.

"Therefore I am going to forgive you on [date]."

Or "I'm not going to forgive you, and the cost of not forgiving will be

_____.

_____.

Now, make a contract for forgiving yourself by filling in the blanks:

I will forgive myself on [date] for [whatever I did] even if [another person's name] is unwilling to forgive me.

If I am not willing to [define action], then it means I am not willing to forgive and I am still holding resentment against myself and/or others.

If I *am* willing to do this, I can then begin to trust myself to
[define action].

From Satisfaction to Joy

When people hope and trust, they expect things to turn out all right and they expect to experience satisfaction, pleasure, and enjoyment. Words such as *enjoyment* and *pleasure* are often used interchangeably. Words such as *satisfaction* and *joy* are not. Satisfaction is not as strong as pleasure or joy. People may only *hope* for satisfaction and wish and want pleasure. They *long* for joy.

Satisfactions are often associated with physical needs being met. When these needs are met, the body experiences a homeostasis, a state of physiological equilibrium. "I'm satisfied" is a frequent comment made after eating an adequate meal or getting adequate sleep. Feelings of satisfaction may also be experienced in relation to a person's job, or family, or social or economic life. "I'm satisfied with what I've got," such a person might say.

Many people believe satisfaction is a desirable state of being. They may not seek or expect to find anything more. This is especially true of people who are physically or mentally ill. Their expectations are often lowered in proportion to their lowered health. It is often a sign of "getting well" when they begin to seek some form of pleasure. The taste of a favorite food may give pleasure, whereas an adequate meal gives only satisfaction.

The sense of pleasure is a much stronger, more positive feeling than physical satisfaction. Pleasure includes a sense of enjoyment although not the high elation that is part of joy. Pleasure can permeate almost all areas of living, though many people do not allow it to do so.

Although pleasure may be related to physical satisfactions, pleasure is also experienced at an intellectual level, say, for example, when reading an interesting book or having a stimulating conversation. So, too, the sense of pleasure may follow a task well planned or a job well done.

One person's pleasure may be another person's pain. Some people, for example, like certain kinds of music or foods, and other people detest the same music and food. As another example, one person may experience pleasure with sexual relief. To another person it might be pain.

Joy has a much different quality from pleasure. After a pleasurable experience, people often wish or want more. After an experience of joy, they *long* for it; they yearn for it. From the center of being they almost hunger for it, and the hunger is seldom satisfied, except for the moment. The sense of joy does not last; it is transitory, often unexpected. Joy is a sensation or emotion of delight. It is a unique experience. It is often remembered and can sustain and comfort a person throughout life.

Joy may be felt in response to an external dynamic or an internal dynamic. It can be personal or interpersonal, based on achievement or not. At a personal level, when something I am creating turns out "just right," I have a moment of joy in *my* achievement. Or when I work with a colleague or client and the work turns out to be "just right," I experience a sense of interpersonal joy that is not mine—it is *our* achievement. Or when I see the first spring flowers open their lovely faces, I rejoice in *their* "absolutely perfect and just right" achievement.

Joy often goes with pride and pleasure in the achievements of others. What parent or teacher has not been joyful at the success of a child? What friend has not rejoiced at the success of another friend?

Joy is not just in response to achievement. It is often a response to words from other people that alleviate fear and anxiety.

"Don't worry; everything's going to be all right."

"The job is yours if you want it."

"No; the tumor is benign."

So, too, words that speak of love and care often lead to hope and joy:

"Hi, Mom. I'm free now. I'm coming home."

"I love you with all my heart."

Joy is sometimes a transcendent moment that interrupts personal belief structures and habits of behaving that may have been generated during years when defending, attracting, rationalizing, and manipulating seemed to be the only options. Although all people are manipulative at various times, in spite of it joy may break through and brief freedom may be experienced.

When joy is experienced intensely, it often seems to come from the depths of being, and the feeling floods the person. For a moment or so the whole universe seems different, its structure and power awesome, its beauty overpowering. Everything is in harmony in a universal spirit.

Your Experiences of Joy

Sit in a comfortable chair. Unwind your arms and legs. Let the tension in your shoulders go, and let your eyes slowly close halfway.

Let your mind drift back to your own experiences of joy. See yourself once more in situations when you had those transcendent moments.

After you have looked at several scenes, ask yourself what preceded the feeling. What other feelings accompanied the joy? How long did the joy last? What happened as a result?

Notes from a Workshop

Satisfaction, pleasure, and joy are all unique experiences. Different people value them differently.

Carmen, an attractive forty-year-old secretary, was satisfied with the status quo and was very critical of other women in her office who were goal oriented. "I don't see why they work so hard. What do they want to get out of life, anyway? *Why can't they just be satisfied with things as they are* and stop rocking the boat? They make enough to live on, so why should they want 'equal opportunities' and all that stuff?"

Carmen continued, "I'm satisfied with what I've got. When I compare myself to people who have less, I'm even more satisfied. I don't want to get anywhere or change anything—not even me—I just want to stay as I am."

Lucille, a lively mother of three school-age children, disagreed with Carmen's philosophy. She had studied how to be a good parent to herself and was repeating the workshop for further growth and freedom. She said, "Not me. I'm not satisfied. I'm doing OK, but I still want to develop myself more. The way I figure it is that I probably only have one lifetime to live, so I'm going back to school to learn how to think. Another thing I'm going to do is to learn how to play, how to laugh, and how to just enjoy living."

"You see," said Lucille, "I never learned how to play. I was always so busy trying to please my parents and teachers, and my husband and kids, and do what they wanted that there wasn't time. Even now I don't seem to fit into situations where people tell jokes and kind of act silly. I feel very awkward then and socially inept. I think I missed out in childhood in my positive development of social and academic skills. Now with my encouraging new parent, I am sure I can develop both. And I'm going to start by learning how to have fun."

Karl, also in the workshop, was a tall, rather quiet accountant who agreed with Lucille that problem solving was not enough. "I'm like you," he said. "I want to have fun and be able to belly-laugh. I want to enjoy life, not hate it. I want to be able to love my inner child, not destroy it. In other words, I want to live and I want to *enjoy* living, not just *endure* it.

"I think I spoil my own happiness—all by myself. You see, I hassle myself when something goes wrong, and things often 'go wrong' because, although I'm very good in many things, I'm not perfect. So I need a new parent message that says, 'You don't have to be perfect. You need to learn how to play and how to enjoy life.' "

The Importance of Play

As long ago as prehistoric times people probably found opportunity to play. The wall paintings of animals in ancient paleolithic caves at Altamira, Spain, point to the leisure time that must have been available for creativity and "playing around" with design and paint. At a much later date, excavations of many ancient cultures show that children played many games and had many objects to play with. For example, the Aztecs did not have the wheel, yet their animal toys had rollers on the feet of the animals. The bow was seemingly played as a musical instrument long before it was used as a weapon. Obviously prehistoric existence, and all existence since then, has been more than the scramble for survival. Play, creativity, and the expression of both in art, in dance, and in song have always been part of life.

Play is Hope and Joy

Smolan

National Archives

"I hope I make it this time."

"When I grow up I hope I play well."

"I can hardly wait for my turn."

"I hope we'll always have fun like this!"

Stock, Boston, Inc.

Lejeune

Some people live their lives as though work is their only choice. Obviously that's not true. Even people in the most dire circumstances sometimes laugh and play. Not to do so is to become "a *beast* of burden" rather than a human being—perhaps with a burden that can occasionally be put down.

It is not surprising that so many people do not know how to play. There are all too many critical parents who proclaim:

"No play until your work is done."

"Play is the work of the devil."

"Stop playing and get to work."

More nurturing parents see the value of play. They disagree with the concept that work must precede play. They agree with slogans such as, "All work and no play makes Jack a dull boy," and often enjoy playing themselves. If they are knowledgeable parents, they recognize play as the work of a child and that children who play are likely to be more emotionally healthy than those who don't.

Play comes in many forms. Substitute people—dolls such as baby dolls, teenage dolls, Star Wars dolls, and Farmer Jones dolls—all are invitations to experimenting with roles that children may act out when they are adults. Play objects such as cars and trucks, tractors and planes, also add to the creative fantasy life that children naturally experience.

A quite different kind of play emerges as children experiment with physical play. "Splash" goes the water, to the delight of an infant who kicks it. "Swish" goes the birch tree, to the delight of the child who swings on it. "Splat" goes the ball to the delight of the child who hits it with a baseball bat. And so coordination of the body develops, often with play, and it feels good with moments of joy.

One of life's beauties is the capacity to play creatively, and one of the problems many people have when they start to grow up is that they forget how to play, or perhaps never knew how. They become accustomed to a life without silliness, laughter, satisfaction, fantasy, and joy. They settle for achievement and usefulness in nurturing others. They deny themselves the fun and joy of the moment.

Other people, a little more relaxed, are able to play but only do so when they "go out." Their old parent tapes say things such as, "Go outside and play," or "Don't play in the house," or "Don't be noisy." Instead of enjoying themselves at home, these people create excuses for "going out and having some fun." When this becomes the pattern, their marriage or other living arrangement suffers because, in many cases, people spend more time in their homes than outside them. And if being inside is associated with childhood unhappiness, then "going out" may be the only option they are aware of when they get older. The task in such cases is to change the atmosphere *inside* the home to one that contributes to satisfaction and pleasure.

It is in this kind of atmosphere that playfulness and its many forms, including gaiety, humor, exuberance, and laughter, can develop. Playfulness is one of the characteristics of self-actualizing people.

Let's Go Play

Play in some people's minds is associated with laughter; in others it may be associated with fantasy or with experimenting with future life roles, as when "playing house" or "playing doctor."

What was play like for you? Was it pain or pleasure? What kinds of play did you engage in? Where? With whom? How has it affected your life?

Now that you're grown up, how do you play? Where? When? With whom? Do you play enough?

If not, what kind of encouragement for play does your new parent need to give you?

Laughter as a Road to Freedom

Laughter is often an important ingredient in play. It is also therapeutic. It activates the chemistry for the will to live. It reflects joy and insight, attracts friends and lovers, breaks tension in uncomfortable social situations, and seemingly increases the capacity to fight against disease. By expanding the chest, increasing respiration, forcing poisoned air from lung cells, laughter relaxes the body and helps stimulate the balance which is called health.

One of the most dramatic cases of the curative effects of laughter is that of Norman Cousins, distinguished editor of the *Saturday Review*, who says that, in part, he laughed his way out of the hospital and out of a very serious, crippling collagen illness that doctors believed to be irreversible. He refused to give up.

In many ways Norman Cousins took responsibility for his cure and got the cooperation of his attending physician to use nontraditional techniques for curing him. Today, some years later, he remains cured and fully active, physically, as well as intellectually. One of the curative techniques Cousins used was laughter.

It's not easy to laugh when hurting, yet Cousins secured a movie projector and humorous TV films from the series "Candid Camera" and watched them and laughed. Cousins also turned to books of humor for further fun. The positive effect was cumulative. Laughter, he decided, was good medicine and essential for his health.

Laughter is also used in psychotherapy. Victor Frankl, originator of logotherapy, which is therapy to discover meaning, used laughter to treat persons with phobias or obsessive/compulsive patterns. He claimed that a person "develops a sense of detachment toward his neurosis by laughing at it." To facilitate this sense, patients are encouraged to exaggerate their symptoms rather than use energy fighting against the symptoms or avoiding situations in which the anxiety would arise. It works. Seeing how ridiculous a neurosis is in the light of reality often leads to an Adult "aha" laugh of insight and a shout of joyful laughter from the Child because of the new-found freedom. As Eric Berne, the originator of transactional analysis and ego state theory wrote: ". . . the road to freedom is through laughter, and until he learns that, man will be enslaved, either subservient to his masters or fighting to serve under a new master." In my own work as a psychotherapist I enjoy using laughter for breaking free.

The Importance of Work

Work is often important for survival, yet many people do not interpret their work as being important if it is *only* for survival purposes. Work that gives personal satisfaction or pleasure is what is seen as important by the person doing it.

A mechanic may be satisfied with the work done on a car or may even experience pleasure at being able to find the cause of a knock in the engine. Another mechanic may have only negative feelings because of having to work to eat. Someone who is cleaning house may be satisfied, even experience pleasure, when the task is completed. Another person could be

Laugh and the World Laughs with You

James

Stock, Boston, Inc.

"C'mon in. The water's fine."

"Laughter cures."

Stock, Boston, Inc.

"I like the way we work together."

"Wow, you're funny."

Stock, Boston, Inc.

quite indifferent if neither the process of working nor the results of the work are seen as important.

Sometimes specific tasks present major challenges. If the challenges are met and conquered, persons doing so may even feel a surge of joy. Hope and will have been motivating factors; senses of purpose and competence have been their allies. For example, an architect may be challenged by a particular design problem, decide to solve the problem, and feel a flash of pride and joy on reaching the goal. Like a marathon runner who, after putting everything into winning a race, wants to win another, the architect may seek out even more difficult problems to solve.

Like play, learning how to work begins during childhood. The games that children play are often rehearsals for later work. The school's demands for homework and the parents' demands for housework or chores are usually the first experiences of being in the work force. With this emphasis on work, the focus of life often becomes one of doing rather than being.

Some people are so caught up in work that it becomes the focus of their lives. These people are workaholics. Whether a job is a paid or a volunteer one, workaholism is common. A housewife who compulsively polishes and repolishes what is already polished is as addicted as the person who goes to work early, works through the lunch break, and stays late to work. So too is the entrepreneur, the independent consultant, the creative artist. Each may put in incredibly long hours either because they are interested and want to work at their interests or because they feel compelled to do so because of the high goals they have established.

Many workaholics work themselves to a point of exhaustion, even to the point of breaking down physically or emotionally. Only by overworking and collapsing do they feel justified in taking care of themselves. Work is important for these people, yet they often use work as an excuse to avoid being close to others and to avoid being loving parents to themselves. They use their work as a defense against their anxiety. Workaholics may or may not enjoy their work.

Notes from a Workshop

The ability to want some positive caring from somebody else is often accelerated by getting help from someone else. Workaholic Quintin summarized the process as he experienced it:

"I always thought I *had* to work before I could play. Growing up on a farm must have made me like that. So I came to the workshop because I wanted 'permission' so that I would not be so compulsive about completing every task before I could relax and enjoy myself. On my job I was often exploited by being given additional work (if you want the work done, give it to the busy man). The truth is I was a workaholic.

"Then in the workshop I sat on the floor, as you instructed, and my partner was in a chair. My partner asked, 'Quintin, what do you want?' I answered, 'I don't want to have to work after five o'clock.' He kept asking the question. I made the same response. At last he said, 'Quintin, you don't have to work after five o'clock.' The expression of excitement on my face when I finally really heard the permission caused the group to laugh.

"That exercise was so effective I am no longer a workaholic. Recently at work I tried to continue after 5:00 but found that I could only accomplish manual tasks—no serious studying or thinking. I cannot even read professional journals or books after 5:00. It's like having a new script for living. And it happened partly during the exercise of sitting on the floor, feeling really little again and being asked, for the first time, 'Quintin, what do you want?'"

Hope and Work

Spiral back in time to the parent messages you received about work in general and about the kind of work they expected you to do. How have you complied, rebelled, or procrastinated in reference to their expectations?

In your present work, do you have satisfaction or pleasure or moments of joy? What hopes do you have for your work in the future? Do you need to give yourself new parent messages that will put realistic hope into action?

Choosing to Enjoy

Santayana wrote, "There is no cure for birth and death save to enjoy the interval." That's the challenge—to enjoy life between the times of pain.

To do that means taking charge of one's feelings—choosing to enjoy life rather than feel miserable. To do this implies that at any time people can decide what their emotional response to a particular situation can be. Naturally it sometimes seems easier to give in, to be self-indulgent, to cherish negative feelings. At these times people are often *choosing* to be enslaved to their feelings. "I can't help it," they may say. Yet they own their feelings. Their feelings do not own them.

When aware of the temptation to give in to hopelessness, it is useful to bring to mind the four "enjoy" choices as developed by psychologists Robert and Mary Goulding. These are choices anyone can use when faced with the question of whether to do something and what attitude to take to the doing. The choices are:

Do it and enjoy it.

Do it and don't enjoy it.

Don't do it and enjoy it.

Don't do it and don't enjoy it.

To enjoy something is to know pleasure, perhaps even a glimpse of joy. Enjoyment isn't a "peak" feeling, yet it certainly is better than feeling depressed because life seems bleak and disaster seems imminent. Choosing to do things and to enjoy doing them can become a healthy habit. It often needs cultivating.

Your Enjoyment Style

Evaluate what you have been doing the past week or what somebody thought you "ought" to do.

Have you enjoyed doing what you've done?

Have you done it yet *not* enjoyed it?

Have you *not* done it and enjoyed not doing it?

Have you *not* done it and *not* enjoyed the not doing?

On a scale of 1 to 10 (10 being high), what has been your enjoyment style recently? Do you need to develop new parent messages for more enjoyment?

From Joy to Happiness

Each moment of joy is like a priceless pearl. Real pearls are found in oysters and although oysters taste good (to some people), they are seldom beautiful; in fact, they are downright slimy. Yet when oyster pearls are cleaned and polished, they are often exhibited to the public on elegant black velvet or around a lovely neck.

So it is with joy. It may be found in an ugly shell, in a slimy situation. And it may occur in elegant situations of beauty. Joy comes like an unexpected and longed-for friend who cannot be bought or sold but only cared for and loved. Transcendent joy is but a moment, a touch of paradise when all the real or imagined angels break out in some kind of hallelujah chorus.

Happiness is not a momentary experience as is joy. It is an ongoing attitude toward life. To be happy is to live by hope in spite of situations that bring neither satisfaction, nor pleasure, nor joy. Happiness involves remembering and cherishing the moments of joy, putting them together like a string of pearls and wearing them freely or holding them prayerfully as though holding a rosary.

Both rosaries and strings of pearls are often strung with knots between each bead. A happy person hopes for and savors the moments of joy, in spite of the unhappy "knots" that occur. An unhappy person, like a pessimist looking at the half-full glass, exaggerates the knots.

Some joys are related to longed-for gifts. I remember the joy of receiving a china-headed doll at age three; a violin at age nine; books that are still special to me, like *Japanese Fairy Tales*, *A Child's Garden of Verses*, *The Little Prince*; a real crystal ball on the basis of a casual remark I made, a hair dryer when I was learning to set my hair when resigning from the Dumb and Ugly Club. I also cherish a little, pink glass elephant from a friend, notes from my children and other friends, love letters from my husband. These and many more led to moments of joy—affirmations that somebody cared. Each joy of the past, when remembered, contributes to my happiness now.

Then there were sensory experiences that brought joy, sometimes awe and wonder: looking up through the branches of a gigantic redwood tree as I stood at its base, watching butterflies as they danced, getting lost in a drop of dew on a pine needle, hearing water bounce over pebbles and rocks, wind whispering through tall branches, fires crackling on the hearth, Chopin as played by my mother, the meadowlarks in the field. And the sweet smell and taste of hot applesauce and the scent of wet leaves on the ground and the pungency of the saltwater spray banging on majestic Seal Rocks in San Francisco, and the touch of the wet sand on my feet, and the tilt of the ferryboat crossing the bay.

Some other special events that also gave my life meaning were family camping, Thanksgiving with relatives while laughing and playing charades, singing around the piano as dinner cooked, whizzing through the streets of San Francisco on roller skates, getting married, giving birth to my children, loving them, through good times and bad, even the surprise when *Born to Win*, the book that Dorothy Jongeward and I coauthored, suddenly began to be translated into so many languages.

And so it goes. Joy is many-faceted. Many moments of past joy and many more in the present now, and still more to come. Of course, I could also list the agonies. Why bother?

Happiness is recognizing that although there are knotty problems in life, like knots between fine pearls, moments of joy are beautiful. Each one can be cherished.

For the Time Being

The "pursuit of happiness" which is based on hope is an inalienable right. It is a given freedom, according to the U.S. Constitution. Please note, happiness itself is *not* a right; the *pursuit* of it is.

Understandably enough, it is not surprising that many people get tired of the pursuit. Chasing after what often seems to be around the corner, then around the next corner, and the next and the next, often becomes tiring—even for a jogger. Most people pursuing something expect or hope to reach it. When day after day, month after month, year after year passes without touching the goal, hope may seem dead. When this is the case, courage is required—courage to go on in spite of seeming hopelessness and distress.

This kind of courage involves both determination and commitment. The commitment is for life. It means maintaining and continuing to develop your new parent so that you live life more abundantly. It means using and practicing your new parenting skills with yourself constantly. This is very important. Don't stop now. Continue to accentuate the positive; eliminate the negative. Like an athlete who exercises to stay in shape, you need the same kind of commitment in choosing a lifetime of breaking free.

The poem by W. H. Auden, "For the Time Being," affirms the process. He writes, "The distress of choice is our chance to be blessed." Being a new loving parent to yourself does not take away the distress that often goes along with making choices. The distress is part of freedom and having the opportunity to make choices is also our chance to be blessed.

To be blessed is to experience joy, to know freedom, to have an inner peace that is sustaining in any and every situation. To know joy is to have a gradual or sudden self-awareness. It is to feel free, alive, and vital, not spellbound, fearful, and anxious. To know joy is to recognize the sense of personal power and to appreciate the power of others without competing for a power position. To know joy is to discover the unlimited capacity of the self for being and doing, for loving, for caring, for sharing, and for commitment. And, for the time being, isn't that enough?

For the Time Being

Hebble

"Take care of yourself."

"Celebrate breaking free."

San Francisco Chronicle

Celebrating Freedom

As this book ends and you go on with your new life, make several plans now for doing something fun, like making mud pies, flying kites, climbing trees, that you haven't done since childhood. Or find a young child and help that child build a treehouse or playhouse or a little theater or something else for fun. Have a costume party. Ring up a friend. Be silly.

Draw a picture of yourself jumping up and down freely or breaking out of a confining situation. Get into a big cardboard box and break through it. Open a window and shout out, "Hello World!" Do it *now.* Do it two or three times. Use different windows or doors. Yell out, "Hi, new Parent! I'm glad I've got you!" Look in a mirror and make faces at yourself.

Stop holding yourself back. Stop beating yourself up. You don't need to spend any more of your life being depressed or resentful or bored. Boredom happens when natural curiosity dies. So get interested in something new. Play. Have fun. It's beautiful to feel, to think, to care, to know joy and happiness. Celebrate your freedom. Celebrate now!

P.S. A Personal Thank-You

I have always been interested in the concept of human freedom. I imagine I always will be. I thank you for sharing this interest. As I said in the first chapter, I have been developing this basic material for many years and have used it with my clients and students, whom I always care for and sometimes love. However, I have most often used it in workshop situations, not in the form presented in this book. Therefore I am very interested in hearing from you.

One of my highest priorities is that my writings be interesting and *useful.* I don't want them to impress people or depress them. I want them to have a positive direction with specific techniques that can be used to solve problems. I believe that as problems are solved, people experience a higher sense of vitality and aliveness, commitment and power, joy and happiness.

Only you can tell me if I have achieved my goals. Therefore please write and let me know what the process has been for you in learning how to be a new loving parent to yourself. Also let me know if you want to attend a self-reparenting workshop.

But I want to thank you, my readers, whether you write to me or not. Without you, the colors would not be so vivid; the sounds would not be so harmonious; the smell, the taste, the touch of life itself would not be as conducive to freedom as it now is.

Certificate of Release

Let it be known that
by breaking free to a new life with
self-reparenting,
the holder of this certificate,
whose name is:

_____

is no longer qualified to be
a member in

THE DUMB AND UGLY CLUB

and is thereby released
from all obligations and privileges.

CONGRATULATIONS!

Muriel James,   Past President

Bibliography

Ackoff, Russell. *Redesigning the Future: A Systems Approach to Social Problems.* New York: John Wiley, 1974.

Adler, Alfred. *Social Interest: A Challenge to Mankind.* London: Faber and Faber, 1938.

Adler, Alfred. *The Individual Psychology of Alfred Adler.* Heinz Ansbacher and Rowens Ansbacher, eds. New York: Harper & Row, 1964.

Ahlstrom, W. M., and R. G. Havinghurst. *Four Hundred Losers.* San Francisco: Jossey-Bass, 1971.

Ansbacher, H. L. "The Adlerian and Jungian Schools." *American Handbook of Psychiatry,* Vol. 1, Silvano Ariete, Ed. New York: Basic Books, 1974.

Arendt, Hannah. *On Violence.* New York: Harcourt, Brace and World, Inc., 1969.

Aries, P. *Centuries of Childhood: A Social History of Family Life.* (R. Baldick, Trans.) New York: Knopf, 1962.

Assagioli, Roberto, M.D. *The Act of Will.* Baltimore: Penguin Books, 1974.

Auden, W. H., and L. Kronenberger, eds. *The Viking Book of Aphorisms.* New York: Viking Press, 1966.

Axline, Virginia. *Dibs: In Search of Self.* New York: Ballantine Books, 1964.

Bandura, A. *Aggression: A Social Learning Analysis.* Englewood Cliffs, N.J.: Prentice-Hall, 1973.

Beard, Mary. *Women As Force in History: A Study in Traditions and Realities.* New York: Macmillan, 1946.

Becker, Ernest. *The Denial of Death.* New York: The Free Press (Macmillan), 1973.

Berne, Eric. *What Do You Say After You Say Hello?* New York: Grove Press, 1971.

Bettelheim, Bruno. *The Empty Fortress.* New York: The Free Press, 1967.

Bettelheim, Bruno. *A Home for the Heart.* New York: Knopf, 1974.

Bickler, Robert. *Child Development: An Introduction* (2nd ed.). Boston: Houghton Mifflin Co., 1981.

Brown, Barbara B. *Supermind: The Ultimate Energy.* New York: Harper & Row, 1980.

Bowlby, John. *Attachment and Loss, Vol. I.* New York: Basic Books, 1969.

Bowlby, John. *Attachment and Loss, Vol. II. Separation, Anxiety and Anger.* New York: Basic Books, 1973.

Buber, Martin. *Between Man and Man.* Boston: Beacon Press, 1955.

Coleman, James. *Power and the Structure of Society.* New York: W. W. Norton & Co., Inc., 1975.

Cousins, Norman. "Anatomy of an Illness (as perceived by the patient)." *New England Journal of Medicine,* 1976, 19458–1463.

Cox, Harvey. *Turning East.* New York: Simon and Schuster, 1977.

DeBeauvoir, Simone. *The Second Sex.* New York: Bantam Books, 1961.

Donaldson, M. *Children's Minds.* New York: Norton, 1979.

Duska, Ronald, and Mariellen Whelan. *Moral Development: A Guide to Piaget and Kohlberg.* New York: Paulist Press, 1975.

Elias, Norbert. *The Civilizing Process: The Development of Manners* (Edmund Jephcott, trans.). New York: Urizen Books, 1978.

Ellenberger, Henri. *The Discovery of the Unconscious: The History and Evolution of Dynamic Psychiatry.* New York: Basic Books, 1970.

Erikson, Erik. *Childhood and Society* (2nd ed.). New York: W. W. Norton, 1963.

Erikson, Erik. "Identity and the Life Cycle." *Psychological Issues, 1,* 1958, monograph 1.

Evans, R. I. *Dialogue with Erik Erikson.* New York: Harper & Row, 1967.

Farber, Leslie. *The Ways of the Will.* New York: Basic Books, 1965.

Flexner, Eleanor. *Century of Struggle.* Cambridge: Belknap Press, Harvard University, 1959.

Fraiberg, Selma. *The Magic Years.* New York: Scribner, 1959.

Frankl, Viktor. *Man's Search for Meaning.* New York: Washington Square Press, 1963.

Frankl, Viktor. *The Doctor and the Soul.* New York: Knopf, 1957.

Freedman, Daniel. "Ethnic Differences in Babies," *Human Nature,* January 1979.

Freud, Anna. *Infants without Families.* New York: International Universities Press, 1944.

Freud, Sigmund. "Analysis, Terminable and Interminable." *Collected Papers,* 5:316. London: Hogarth Press, 1950.

Frieden, Betty. *The Feminine Mystique,* 10th anniversary edition. New York: W. W. Norton, 1974.

Fromm, Erich. *Fear of Freedom.* London: Routledge & Kegan Paul, Ltd., 1942.

Fromm, Erich. *Man for Himself.* Greenwich, Conn.: Fawcett Publications, Inc., 1967.

Fromm, Erich. *The Sane Society.* Greenwich, Conn.: Fawcett Premier, 1955.

Furth, H. *Piaget for Teachers.* Englewood Cliffs, N.J.: Prentice-Hall, 1970.

Ginsburg, H., and S. Opper. *Piaget's Theory of Intellectual Development* (2nd ed.). Englewood Cliffs, N.J.: Prentice-Hall, 1979.

Gould, Roger. "Adult Life Stages: Growth Toward Self Tolerance." *Psychology Today*, February 1975, pp. 74–78.

Gould, Roger. "The Phases of Adult Life: A Study of Developmental Psychology." *American Journal of Psychiatry*, 129:5, November 1972.

Goulding, Mary, and Robert Goulding. *Changing Lives through Redecision Therapy*. New York: Brunner-Mazel, 1979.

Goulding, Robert and Mary Goulding. Four "enjoy" choices. Personal communication.

Green, Elmer and Alyce Green. *Beyond Biofeedback*. Delacorte Press, 1977.

Hammarskjold, Dag. *Markings*. London: Faber & Faber, Ltd., 1964.

Harlow, H. F. *Learning to Love*. New York: Ballantine Books, 1971.

Harlow, H. F. "The Nature of Love." *American Psychologist, 13*, 1958, pp. 673–685.

Herron, R. E., and B. Sutton-Smith. *Child's Play*. New York: Wiley, 1971.

Hesse, Hermann. *Siddhartha*. New York: New Directions, 1951.

Hillary, Edmund. *Nothing Venture, Nothing Win*. New York: Coward, McCann & Geoghegan, 1975.

Hoffer, Eric. *The Passionate State of Mind*. New York: Harper & Row, 1954.

Horney, Karen. *Neurosis and Human Growth*. New York: Norton, 1950.

Horney, Karen. *The Neurotic Personality of Our Time*. New York: Norton, 1937.

James, Muriel. *Born to Love*. Reading, Mass.: Addison-Wesley, 1973.

James, Muriel. *Marriage Is for Loving*. Reading, Mass.: Addison-Wesley, 1979.

James, Muriel. "Self-Reparenting: Theory and Process." *Transactional Analysis Journal* 4:3, July 1974.

James, Muriel. "The Inner Core and the Human Spirit." *Transactional Analysis Journal* 10:1, January 1981.

James, Muriel. *The OK Boss*. Reading, Mass.: Addison-Wesley, 1975.

James, Muriel. "Therapy Doesn't Always Hurt: Laugh Therapy." *Transactional Analysis Journal* 9:4, October 1979.

James, Muriel. *Transactional Analysis for Moms and Dads*. Reading, Mass.: Addison-Wesley, 1974.

James, Muriel, and contributors. *Transactional Analysis for Psychotherapists and Counselors*. Reading, Mass.: Addison-Wesley, 1977.

James, Muriel, and Dorothy Jongeward. *Born to Win: Transactional Analysis with Gestalt Experiments*. Reading, Mass.: Addison-Wesley, 1971.

James, Muriel, and Louis Savary. *A New Self*. Reading, Mass.: Addison-Wesley, 1977.

James, Muriel, and Savary, Louis M. *The Heart of Friendship*. New York: Harper & Row, 1976.

Kagan, J. *Developmental Studies of Reflection and Analysis*. Cambridge, Mass.: Harvard University Press, 1964.

Kohlberg, L., and E. Turiel, eds. *Recent Research in Moral Development*. New York: Holt, Rinehart & Winston, 1972.

Kohlberg, Lawrence. "From Is to Ought." In J. Mischel ed. *Cognitive Development and Epistemology.* New York: Academic Press, 1971.

Kohlberg, Lawrence. "Stage and Sequence: The Cognitive Developmental Approach to Socialization." In D. Goslin ed. *Handbook of Socialization Theory and Research.* New York: Rand McNally, 1969.

Laing, R. D. *The Divided Self.* Middlesex, England: Tavistock Publishing, Penguin Books, 1965.

Laing, Raven. *The Birth Book.* Palo Alto, Calif.: Genesis, 1972.

Lamaze, Fernand. *Painless Childbirth: The Lamaze Method.* Chicago: Contemporary Books, 1970.

Lamb, M. E., ed. *The Role of the Father in Child Development.* New York: Wiley, 1976.

Leboyer, Frederick. *Birth Without Violence.* New York: Knopf, 1975.

Lickona, T., ed. *Moral Development and Behavior: Theory, Research, and Social Issues.* New York: Holt, Rinehart, & Winston, 1976.

Lorenz, K. *On Aggression.* New York: Harcourt, Brace and World, 1966.

Lynd, Helen Merrill. *On Shame and the Search for Identity.* New York: Science Editions, 1966.

Machlowitz, Marilyn. *Workaholics.* Reading, Mass.: Addison-Wesley, 1980.

Madruga, Lenor. *One Step at a Time.* New York: McGraw-Hill, 1979.

Maier, Henry. *Three Theories of Child Development.* New York: Harper & Row, 1965.

Maslow, Abraham. *Motivation and Personality* (2nd ed.). New York: Harper & Row, 1970.

Maslow, Abraham. *The Further Reaches of Human Nature.* New York: Viking, 1972.

Maslow, Abraham. *Toward a Psychology of Being* (2nd ed.). Princeton, N.J.: D. Van Nostrand Co., 1968.

Masters, William, and Virginia Johnson. *Human Sexual Inadequacy.* Boston: Little, Brown, 1967.

May, Rollo. *Love and Will.* New York: W. W. Norton, 1969.

May, Rollo. *Power and Innocence: A Search for the Sources of Violence.* New York: W. W. Norton, 1972.

Milgram, Stanley. *Obedience to Authority.* New York: Harper & Row, 1974.

Miller, N., and J. Dollard. *Social Learning and Imitation.* New Haven: Yale University Press, 1941.

Montagu, Ashley. "Constitutional and Prenatal Factors in Infant and Child Health." In *Human Development,* Morris Haimowitz and Natalie Haimowitz, eds., 3rd ed. New York: Thomas Crowell Co., 1973.

Montagu, Ashley. *Life Before Birth.* New York: New American Library, Signet Books, 1965.

Moody, Raymond, Jr. *Laugh After Laugh.* Jacksonville, Fla.: Headwaters Press, 1978.

Mueller, J. Theodore, trans. *Luther's Commentary on Genesis.* Grand Rapids, Mich.: Zondervan, 1958.

Muus, R. *Theories of Adolescence* (3rd ed.). New York: Random House, 1975.

Piaget, Jean. *The Construction of Reality in the Child.* New York: Basic Books, 1954.

Piaget, Jean. *The Moral Judgement of the Child.* New York: Harcourt, Brace, 1932; Collier Books Edition, 1962.

Piaget, Jean. *The Origin of Intelligence in Children.* New York: International University Press, 1952.

Piaget, Jean. *The Psychology of Intelligence.* London: Routledge and Kegan Paul Ltd., 1950.

Rokeach, Milton. *The Nature of Human Values.* New York: Free Press, 1973.

Rothenberg, Albert. "Creative Contradictions." *Psychology Today,* June 1979.

Samuels, Mike, M.D. and Nancy Samuels. *Seeing with the Mind's Eye.* New York: Random House, 1975. *Self,* June 1980.

Selye, Hans. *Stress without Distress.* Philadelphia: J. B. Lippincott, 1974.

Selye, Hans. *The Stress of Life.* New York: McGraw-Hill, 1973.

Shaw, Nancy Stoller. *Forced Labor.* Elmsford, N.Y.: British Books Center, 1974.

Sheehy, Gail. *Passages: Predictable Crises in Adult Life.* New York: E. P. Dutton, 1976.

Simonton, O. Carl., M.D.; Stephanie Matthews-Simonton; and James Creighton. *Getting Well Again.* Los Angeles: J. P. Tarcher, Inc., 1978.

Spitz, R. A. *The First Year of Life.* New York: International Universities Press, 1965.

Sprinthall, Richard, and Norman Sprinthall. *Educational Psychology: A Developmental Approach.* Reading, Mass.: Addison-Wesley, 1974.

Stark, R., and J. McEvoy. "Middle Class Violence." *Psychology Today,* 4, 1970, pp. 52–65.

Stern, D. *The First Relationship: Mother and Infant.* Cambridge, Mass.: Harvard University Press, 1977.

Sullivan, Harry Stack. *The Fusion of Psychiatry and Social Science.* New York: W. W. Norton, 1964.

Terkel, Studs. *Working.* New York: Pantheon Books (Random House), 1972, 1974.

Terman, L. M., and M. Oden. *Genetic Studies of Genius: The Gifted Group at Mid-Life. Thirty-Five Years Followup of the Superior Child.* Stanford, Calif.: Stanford University Press, 1954.

Theobald, Robert. *Habit and Habitat.* New Jersey: Prentice Hall, 1972.

Thomas, Alexander, and Stella Chess. *Temperament and Development.* New York: Brunner/Mazel, 1977.

Thomas, Alexander; Stella Chess; and Herbert G. Birch. *Temperament and Behavior Disorders in Children.* New York: New York University Press, 1969.

Thoreau, Henry David. *Walden II: Where I Lived and What I Lived For.* Quoted by Berger Evans, *Dictionary of Quotations.* New York: Avenal Books, 1978.

Tillich, Paul. *The Courage to Be.* London: Fontana Library, 1952.

Toffler, Alvin. *Future Shock.* New York: Random House, 1970.

Toffler, Alvin. *The Third Wave.* New York: Wm. Morrow, 1980.

von Buddenbrock, Wolfgang. *The Senses.* Ann Arbor: University of Michigan Press, 1970.

Wheelis, Alan. "Will and Psychoanalysis." *Journal of the American Psychoanalytical Association*, 2 April 1956.

Wolman, Benjamin, ed. *Dictionary of Behavioral Science.* New York: Van Nostrand Reinhold Co., 1973.

Zukav, Gary. *The Dancing Wu Li Masters: An Overview of the New Physics.* New York: Wm. Morrow, 1979.

Index

Adaptations, 108, 125, 132, 146, 149
  to authority, 67, 73–77, 79, 83, 87,
    107, 128, 131
Addiction, xxiii, 203
  to life-styles, 79–80
Adler, Alfred, 171
Adolescence, 155, 165, 168
Adoption, 55
  and roots, 36
Adult ego state: 29, 30, 32, 40, 93, 112,
    115, 124, 126, 127, 128, 139, 144,
    147, 166, 175, 183, 184, 201
"Adult leveling position," 110
Anger, 4, 13, 29, 62, 74, 85, 104, 107,
    121, 172, 173, 179, 192
Anxiety, 5, 13, 110, 120, 134, 153, 201,
    203
Authority
  adaptations to, 73–77, 87, 107
  (awareness exercise), 71, 73
  obedience to, 70–71, 83
  parental, xxiii, 67–69
  rebellion against, 74–76
Autogenic training, 110
Autonomy, 4, 15, 32, 41–42, 43, 113,
    130, 145, 146, 153, 156, 166, 168,
    175
Awareness. *See* Self-awareness
Awareness exercise, 10, 22–23, 28–29,
    45, 49, 57–58, 61, 71, 73, 76, 79,
    97–98, 102, 105, 107, 109, 110, 112,
    119–120, 121, 124–125, 130,
    134–135, 136–137, 144, 146–147,
    149, 169, 171–172, 173, 181, 191,
    192, 193–194, 196, 200, 204, 205,
    206

Behavior, compulsive, xxiii, 47, 49, 80,
    113, 132, 146, 191, 203, 204
Biofeedback, 110
Birch, Herbert, 23
"Brainstorming," 145
Brainwashing, 5, 46, 52, 59
Breaking free, xx, xxii, xxiii, xxiv, 6, 13,
    14, 15, 17, 20, 23, 28, 36, 81, 82, 85,
    87, 94, 99, 105, 108, 112, 113, 114,
    116, 134, 142, 145, 175, 180, 187,
    188, 189, 201, 208, 211
Breakthrough exercises, xxi
  awareness and freedom, 17, 19–20
  breaking through with creativity,
    162–164
  comparing life-styles, 87–88, 90–91
  diagnosing your own parents, 63–65
  the needs of the child, 114–116
  personality styles of parents, 38–40
  setting contracts, 183–186
  you and your power, 138–139

Care, 142, 151, 156, 179, 180
Caring, 122, 193, 203
  (awareness exercise), 181
  price of, 179–181
Change, xx, xxi, xxiii, 4, 5, 7, 75, 88,
    172, 173, 175, 181

Caring (cont.)
  (awareness exercise), 173
  and power, 117, 119, 122, 168,
    182
  See also Contracts
Chess, Stella, 23
Child ego state, 29, 30, 32, 33, 34, 40,
    124, 126, 127, 128, 145, 147, 175,
    183, 185, 201
Children
  and cognitive development, 131–132
  and developmental conflicts,
    151–155, 158
  and moral development, 83–86, 87
  and negative messages, 41, 43, 50, 52,
    54–57
  and positive messages, 43, 52
  and temperament styles, 23, 24–25, 27
Cognitive development, 131–132, 134,
    144
  (awareness exercise), 134–135
Compliance. *See* Obedience
Conditioning, 47, 49, 52, 59, 71
Conflicts, developmental, 149, 151,
    152–156, 162
Contracting, process of, 173–177
Contracts, xxiii, 15, 165, 166, 173–177,
    179, 180, 183, 184, 185, 186, 192,
    193, 194
  (awareness exercise), 181
  costs of, 173, 175, 179–181
  revision of, 179
  sabotage of, 174, 176, 177, 179, 184,
    185
Cousins, Norman, 200, 201
Creativity, xxiii, 74, 80, 142, 144–145,
    147, 149, 151, 158–159, 161, 162,
    197, 199
  (awareness exercise), 146–147
  and developmental conflicts, 151
  and intuition, xxiii, 74, 145, 146, 147
  and logical thinking, 144, 145, 147,
    149
"Cultural parent," 58–59, 61
"Cultural scripting," 59, 61, 62
Cultural spells
  (awareness exercise), 61

DeBono, Edward, 147
Depression, 13, 77, 120, 121, 152, 205
"Drivers," 73–74, 80
  addiction to, 74
Drug abuse, 155
Drugs, 79, 80, 99, 182

Ego state theory, 201
Ego states, 29, 38, 184
Enjoyment, 205
  (awareness exercise), 205–206
Erikson, Erik, 149
Ethics, 82, 83

Forgiveness, 192–193
  (awareness exercise), 193–194
Frankl, Victor, 201
Freedom, xxii, 1, 4–5, 7. 16, 17, 19, 41,
    43, 74, 94, 95, 122, 125, 127, 130,
    132, 145, 149, 151, 156, 165, 166,
    168, 173, 174, 181, 182, 189, 193,
    196, 208, 210
  avoidance of, 80–82
Future
  (awareness exercise), 109
Futurology, 108

Gestalt therapy, 110
  (awareness exercise), 110, 112
Goals, xxiii, 13, 56, 57, 120, 154, 165,
    168, 176, 177, 179, 192, 196, 203
  (awareness exercise), 181
  See also Contracts
Good parent, xix, xxii, 7, 9, 11, 13,
    15–16, 21, 32, 34, 70, 79, 88, 93, 98,
    129, 158, 161, 166, 174, 179, 182,
    196
Goulding, Mary, 52
Goulding, Robert, 52
Growth, xix, xx, xxii, 98, 165, 169
  and unmet needs, 95, 99
Guilt, 13, 107, 121, 126, 153, 154, 158,
    179, 180, 181, 189

Happiness, 14, 206–207, 208, 210
Health, 30, 124, 125, 135, 189, 194, 200,
    201

and breaking free, 13
holistic, 136
Holistic theory, 112, 135, 145
Hope, 6, 142, 149, 152, 153, 158, 187,
  188, 189, 191–192, 193, 194, 195,
  203, 206
  (awareness exercise), 191, 192
Hypnotism, 46, 47, 52, 59

Ideal parent, 10, 11, 19, 35, 169, 172, 183
  (awareness exercise), 10
Identity, 1, 145, 156
  development of, 155, 165
Illness, 5, 122, 124, 125, 128, 189, 194
  (awareness exercise), 124–125
  See also Stress
Injunctions, xxiii, 41, 68, 69, 154
  (awareness exercise), 57–58
  negative, 52, 54–57
  See also Spells
Inner child, 15, 30, 51, 52, 93, 110, 112,
  113, 114, 115, 122, 127, 128, 146,
  159, 173, 174, 175, 182, 189, 197
Inner parent, 9, 11, 12, 13, 29, 61, 79,
  91, 112, 125, 158, 159, 189

Journal, xxi, 20, 40, 65, 91, 116, 139,
  164, 186
Joy, xxii, xxiii, 1, 6, 15, 74, 112, 176,
  187, 194, 195, 196, 199, 200, 204,
  205, 206, 207, 208, 210
  (awareness exercise), 196
  and happiness, 206
  and pleasure, 194, 195, 196
  and satisfaction, xxiv, 194, 196, 199

Kahler, Tabie, 73
Kohlberg, Lawrence, 83, 87

Lateral thinking, 147, 149
  (awareness exercise), 149
Laughter, 200–201
  in psychotherapy, 201
Logotherapy, 201
Love, 57, 94, 142, 151, 156, 182
Love, longing for, 9–10
  (awareness exercise), 10

Manipulation, 4, 67, 77, 80, 119, 181,
  196
Maslow, Abraham, 98, 99
Meaning, search for, 1–2, 5, 155
Meditation, 110, 136
Memories, 105–107, 113, 163
  (awareness exercise), 107
Messages, 41, 50, 52, 54, 55, 69, 109,
  113, 172
  and the new parent, 87, 91, 112, 114,
  191, 204, 206
Milgram, Stanley, 70
Moral development, 83–85, 87, 152
Morals, 82, 83, 87, 90

Needs, 93–95, 97, 120, 142, 169
  (awareness exercise), 97–98, 102
  and stress, 104
  system of, 98–99, 101–102
  unmet, 95, 97, 120
  and wants, 94–95, 114, 116, 184
New parent, xxiii, 11, 15, 32, 79, 94, 98,
  107, 109, 116, 124, 125, 132, 142,
  145, 147, 158, 161, 164, 165, 166,
  173, 174, 176, 181, 182, 183, 189,
  197, 200, 208
  and stress reduction, 112–114
Nurturing, 94, 122, 124, 126, 127, 129,
  152, 168, 173, 199

Obedience, xxiii, 30, 70–71, 73, 75, 77,
  82, 83, 85, 87, 90, 107, 108, 119,
  128, 131, 132, 146, 204
  addiction to, 80
  (awareness exercise), 71, 73
  to parents, 7, 30, 55, 67–69, 73
  styles of, 73–74

Parapsychology, 136
Parent ego state, 29, 30, 32, 33, 34, 40,
  63, 65, 73, 124, 126, 127, 128, 139,
  173, 175, 184
Parent figures, xxiii, 29, 32, 40, 52, 63,
  65, 71, 94, 107, 124, 143
Parent power, 67–69, 75
Parent substitutes, 6, 14, 15, 43, 93, 168,
  193

Parental messages, 41, 87, 109, 204
Parenting, xxii, xxiii, 38, 39, 71, 94, 162, 173
Parenting styles, xxii, 15, 32–34, 38–40
Parents, xxi, xxii, 6, 7, 9–10, 14, 22, 42, 43, 47, 63, 67, 68, 73, 87, 97, 124, 143, 144, 146, 171, 182, 192, 193, 199, 203
  and temperament style, 23, 24–25, 27
Perls, Fritz, 110
Personality, xxii, 16, 21, 23, 29, 30, 36, 126, 174
  and kinds of power, 126–129, 139, 171
Personality power, xxiii
  See also Power, personal
Piaget, Jean, 131
Play, 197, 199, 204, 210
  (awareness exercise), 200
  in adults, 61, 197, 199, 200
  in childhood, 6, 55, 199–200, 203
  and laughter, 200
Power, 117, 119, 168, 174, 175, 183
  (awareness exercise), 130
Power, intellectual, xxiii, 117, 126, 128
Power, loss of, 120–121
  (awareness exercise), 121
Power, natural, 126, 128, 129, 166
Power, nurturing, 126
Power, personal, 15, 74, 76, 119, 122, 134, 189, 208
  (awareness exercise), 119–120
  types of, 126–129, 138, 139
Power, physical, xxiii, 117, 122
Power, sources of
  (awareness exercise), 130
Power, spiritual, xxiii, 117, 135–136, 139
  (awareness exercise), 136–137
  and holistic techniques, 135, 136
Prayer, 136
Problem solving
  (awareness exercises), 134–135
Procrastination, xxiii, 6, 30, 32, 67, 70, 71, 75, 76–77, 79, 83, 90, 107, 108, 128, 131, 132, 161, 168, 177, 204

addiction to, 79–80
  (awareness exercise), 79

Rebellion, xxiii, 4, 29, 30, 67, 71, 74–76, 77, 82, 83, 107, 108, 128, 131, 132, 166, 204
  addiction to, 80
  (awareness exercise), 76
Reparenting, 13, 14, 15, 49, 93, 94, 99, 124, 135, 139, 142, 163
Repression, 107, 169
Roots, 35, 36–38

Self-actualization, 16, 98, 102, 119, 126, 127, 156, 200
Self-awareness, 1, 4, 15, 17, 43, 67, 93, 94, 138, 174
Self-doubt, 146, 153, 166, 168, 175
Self-esteem, 14, 16, 46, 52, 54, 68, 101, 121, 126, 143, 182
Self-image, 21, 22, 50, 52, 57, 71, 80
  (awareness exercise), 22–23
Self-reparenting, xix, xxii, xxiii, 9, 10, 11, 13–15, 49, 52, 69, 87, 93, 104, 105, 106, 107, 109, 114, 126, 127, 164, 168, 182, 183, 192, 210, 211
Selye, Hans, 104
Sickness. *See* Illness
Spells, 41–43, 45, 46, 49, 52, 56, 58, 59, 61, 62, 113, 151
  (awareness exercise), 45, 49
  See also Injunctions
Strengths, development of, xxiii, 15, 149, 151–156, 163, 164
  See also Virtues
Stress, xxiii, 93, 94, 95, 105, 110, 114, 120
  (awareness exercise), 105
  and the future, 108–109
  and memories, 105–107
  and the present, 109–110
  reduction of, 93, 112–114
  and unmet needs, 104
  See also Illness
Stress reaction, 104, 108

Television, 61, 155
  and hypnotism, 46
Temperament, xxii, 21, 23, 29, 30, 36
  (awareness exercise), 28–29
  styles of, 23, 24–25, 27–28
Thomas, Alexander, 23
Toffler, Alvin, 108
Transactional analysis (TA), xx, 29, 30, 59, 201
Trust, 6, 42, 57, 94, 131, 142, 152, 156, 165, 174, 194
  (awareness exercise), 193–194
  and forgiveness, 192–193

Value clarification, 83
Values, 15, 74, 80, 82, 83, 87, 155, 180
Vertical thinking, 147, 149
  (awareness exercise), 149

Virtues, 15, 142, 149, 158, 164
  See also Strengths, development of
Visualization, 108
Vitality. See Power, personal

Watts, Alan, xx
Will, 141, 142, 145, 149, 153, 158, 165, 166, 168–169, 171, 175, 189, 203
  (awareness exercise), 169
Will-to-power, 171
  (awareness exercise), 171–172
Wishes, 142, 168
  (awareness exercise), 144
  in childhood, 142–143
Work, 60–61, 112, 201, 203, 204
  (awareness exercise), 204
  in childhood, 55, 203
Workaholics, 153, 203, 204